What Shines

Also by Sydney Lea

What Shines

Sydney Lea

Four Way Books
Tribeca

In loving memory of my friend Stephen Arkin

Library of Congress Cataloging-in-Publication Data

Names: Lea, Sydney, 1942- author.
Title: What shines : poems / by Sydney Lea.
Identifiers: LCCN 2023004564 (print) | LCCN 2023004565 (ebook) | ISBN
9781954245587 (trade paperback) | ISBN 9781954245594 (ebook)
Subjects: LCGFT: Poetry.
Classification: LCC PS3562.E16 W47 2023 (print) | LCC PS3562.E16 (eb-
ook)
| DDC 811/.54--dc23/eng/20230206
LC record available at https://lccn.loc.gov/2023004564
LC ebook record available at https://lccn.loc.gov/2023004565

This book is manufactured in the United States of America and printed on
acid-free paper.

Four Way Books is a not-for-profit literary press. We are grateful for the assistance
we receive from individual donors, public arts agencies, and private foundations
including the New York State Council on the Arts, a state agency.

PROUD MEMBER

[clmp]

We are a proud member of the Community of Literary Magazines and Presses.

Contents

Spring Poem in a Time of Plague

Last night, our pond reclaimed a foot from its ice.
New water winks dark green, and redwings shriek
From reed and shrub. It's good to be out. Two boys
Hike by at "social distance." Each young leaf

Twitches like a springtime chipmunk's ear.
The road's mud grasps at boot-soles while I walk
The other way. On a tree I detect the scar
Of an errant winter driver. I catch the talk

Of these school kids out of school—classmates, admired
Or otherwise, the names of favorite games
They can't play now. The ragged runt defers
To his big companion, who, unprompted, screams

Disdain for all constraints. They pass from hearing.
I note an earthworm turning proper pink.
Soon enough the landscape will be wearing
Seasonal raiment: nodding grass and dank,

Deep moss, spare overlay of meadow flowers.
But I know enough to expect odd snow-squalls, slapped
To anger by nasty winds. We'll see more hours
In which we're sealed in rooms foursquare and flat.

We'll dream perhaps of the past, or pray for the future
When a softer time will come—and go—and mist
Will rise from pond and outlet brook to wander
Down to a busy playground. Sun once kissed

My body at play and sweet bijoux of sweat
Blended with uninfected morning's odor.
Who knew that what our elders labeled older
Meant this strange state? Not then but then not yet.

I. Augury

1949

In the photograph, they're both grinning straight at the Kodak,
An elm, not blighted yet to death, at their backs.

It's years since either parent was on hand.
How did it happen? I'm just past 79.

We live our lives, Psalm 90 says, *as a tale
That is told.* From where I stand, that's all too real.

What startles me is that the tale's so short,
An instant, it seems, from this moment back to its start.

With what I've known, you'd think there'd be chapter on chapter:
Five children, all those grandsons, those granddaughters.

And I *could* go on and on about each one.
But on and on's no longer what it's been.

I have another photo on my dresser,
My mother alone in that one, standing by water

That sluggishly slides by our cabin in Sumneytown.
I don't know how to explain why I can't be found

In the shot. After all, the bucket at her feet
Is full of sunfish I've plucked from that very creek.

Or is it? Like anyone else, I tell myself stories.
Maybe my claim's no more than imaginary,

Which makes it, for me at least, not a bit less true.
The fish are green and orange. Their lips are blue.

I feel the heat that caroms off streamside boulders,
I can whiff the swamp nearby where algae molder.

Who dwells in our old house these days? Search me.
Whose room was mine? Who recalls the ghost elm tree?

The grass in the meadow's likely gone brown as ever.
No pumpkinseed in the pail still gasps or quivers.

Who visits the cabin? Who hooks small fish in the water?
My mother stands there beaming beside my treasures.

I shouldn't be, and yet somehow I'm stunned:
Even the fish in that yellowed photo are young.

HiFi

I think both little sisters
were still too young for school,
we brothers not many years older.

I suspect that what I say is
more than a bit sentimental
and may not have a basis

in anything real back then.
So be it. But let me keep it:
the five of us hearing the tune,

the strings and horns so *alive*.
It's good to be where we are,
near our parents' new HiFi,

which spills into every corner.
The *fidelity*—almost shocking.
They've told us about its wonders,

and now at last they own one.
Having adjusted some knob,
they stand stone-still for a moment,

as if in a sort of trance.
Of course they're both long gone,
so of course they no longer dance,

cheeks touching—or anyhow—
but as long as I say so they do.
Indeed the song I hear now

is precisely "Cheek to Cheek."
Now why would it talk about *swimming
in a river or a creek?*

Or maybe it's actually *fishing*.
Who cares? Strange bliss pours forth
as long as the record keeps spinning.

Sickness, regret, and death
will all arrive in time.
And rancor. I won't forget

the rancor. This evening, however,
we brothers and sisters watch,
enchanted, five children together

on the couch with the fancy lace
while our faithful parents glide
in what looks like a fond embrace.

Augury

I can't explain, but it's true.
At ten years old, I beheld the lemon and slate
of the slender fish, flashing below the surface.
My father told me to settle back:
my gawking over the gunwale rocked our canoe,
E.M. White Guide's Model with feathered hull-planks,
the one he called a work of art.

It is. I have it now.
I'd taken a minnow—or I should say that he had—
from the bait pail, which I called a cage.
I'd run the hook—or rather he had—through a dorsal
and then cast feebly. Five yards, maybe six.
The bobber shivered. *Yank!* yelled my father.
I set the hook and the world took on a meaning

it had never had.
I know. What a claim. I know.
But that's how it felt:
a thrill, but also something like trauma.
That's how it felt.
No, I can't explain.
The only way—and did I really want this?—

to reel the new world back to something
I could grasp would be to bring in my catch.
Easy after all.
I'd learn in time a pickerel's not a prize,
not to so-called serious anglers.
The fish made a thrilling rush
toward a spread of pads, just then folding their lilies,

but then it came back, almost docile,
to the long-handled net that awaited.
My father used forceps to pull the hook,
for fear of the menacing teeth.
An evening star stole out.
Mist began to sheathe the shore.
It swaddled the dockside pine in a gown.

I could just discern the eyes of the fish,
like tiny shards of china.
I dreamed I'd glimpsed my future years,
rife with exploits and color.
Why would a child fetch up such a ludicrous vision?
I'm not the one to answer.
And yet, however tame my life has been,

compared to many, at least,
I believe that vatic moment held some truth.
Oh, I'd catch bigger, better fish.
I'd know all manner of grander things.
But the pickerel gleams to this day
in the hands of that generous parent.
Full dark looming, he gave it back to the lake.

What Shines?

—for my sister Jane

Astonishing, this never-ending effort
to have had a happy childhood. Why does it matter
now, why will yourself into all that forgetting?
She may have been a good mother—at least she tried.

Or did she? Once again, you're the one who's trying.
You contend you do remember moments that glow:
you picture her standing one day in the snow, her teeth
in a chatter, no doubt, and yet she looked quite cheerful—

or she seemed to be trying. As you are. The teeth at least
were one good feature, radiant to the end.
You were poised at the top of a hill on a Flexible Flyer,
red sled that shone, your Christmas present at nine.

It may have brought you joy. You're trying to alter
the down-slope rush, to make it shiny too,
to blot out the icicles of snot, the raw
fingers, chilblains. Pain. A father was there,

a good man, you're quite sure, who's now no more
than a specter, whose presence is no more advantageous
than on that day. Or was it of some avail?
You can't remember. You honestly can't remember.

Perhaps you just don't want to. You're doing well—
at least you're trying—with this, your obstinate bid
to sweep off misfortune, to see if there's anything more
than only sorrow. Well, there were certain instants.

You say, *I remember stones.* You say, *I saw*
a beach by moonlight. And did those pebbles glint
like stars, as you insist? You yearn to be sure
clouds never came to eclipse them. You keep on trying.

There's that pervasive gleam along the shore.
Then you take a step and suddenly there's nothing

Still Life: Interior

It is not me I'd wish
this forsaken barn

to contain, this shell become
over time translucent:

pale light allowed to break
through siding boards

as frail as lacewings. *Now,*
I resolve, like the poet,

I'll do nothing but listen. But sounds?
Not one arrives.

No hooves stir mildewed straw,
for instance. The roof

doesn't creak as it bellies down
nor does it encase

clouds of steam—the redolent
breath of cattle.

If only a poem could be written
to render, or summon,

a rebirth here: that coon hide
might be reclaimed

from mice, again might cloak a body
long since laid bare.

If only hay bales could moisten once more
high in the mow;

or gaskets grow plump in the pump,
restored from dryness,

like sea stars rescued from sand
by a tidal surge;

or skating insects gather
their shadows back

to the stock trough, filled
with the old cold water.

Stitched Together

After some seven decades,
The symmetrical look of the wound—
Its stitches' inch-long grid
Of orderly dots and lines—
Remains completely at odds
With the gash my father made.

The odor of charring meat
Had been drifting up to my nose,
The world felt fresh all around me
With its resonance: grating toads,
Peeper-chant swelling toward dusk,
Distinctive symphony.

Dad cut between index and thumb
And managed to jimmy his mouth
Over that cavity
To draw the venom out.
They say not to do that these days,
But the scar, as I say, if not lovely,

Looks so neat it belies its occasion:
Late afternoon, April-warm,
My father tending his cookfire

Down by the edge of the pond.
I'd been climbing a glacial erratic,
Proud of my strength and valor,

As I vainly considered them then.
I found footholds on that boulder,
And handholds. At last I laid
Those very left-hand fingers
On a shelf at its top, where a jab
Came from nowhere. A copperhead

Had been shucking its torpor in sun.
It was otherworldly, that hurt.
Something just got me! I cried,
Then fell to the sodden earth,
Which must have been less far down
Than my pride had let me surmise.

Next came the dirt-road rush
To a nondescript house in Green Lane
Where the doctor gave me a shot.
In bed by midafternoon,
I felt my neck go rigid
And wry until the light

Of day, colored like lilac,
Sifted through window curtains.
My father leaned over the bed.
He seemed the very emblem
Of love, so my body relaxed
When he put a hand on my head.

Now the water glass on the nightstand,
Dad's dog-eared issue of *Time*
On a chair, the mirror, the knob
Of the door—all struck me as signs
Of a brand-new, glorious beauty.
Under gauze, my left hand throbbed,

But in some striking way I foresaw
That my scar would forever mean
I'd known glory. I couldn't have figured
Just why, and of course never dreamed
It would do so right up to this age:
That is, two decades older

Than my father the winter he died.
Back then, old age felt as distant
As an undiscovered planet.

So the splendor I sought surely wouldn't
Be found by my simply enduring.
Yet whatever I may have imagined,

I find glory now precisely
In how I contain a life,
Whatever its poisons, its riches.
Odors and sounds and sights,
The love of a father and *as* one
Are somehow implied by these stitches.

The Poet's Version

To prompt myself, I remember
cock pheasants that gleam under sun,
mid-Pennsylvania, December,
and me, a young boy with gun.

Likewise Amory Harris.
The two of us crept on all fours.
We clung to the rim of the forest;
our stalk seemed to go on for hours.

This happened so long ago
I'm sure I can make it sound right,
how *emphatic* they looked, those two birds in snow,
totemic against the cold white.

Let my tense be the present: In sunshine,
bright feathers shift and blend.
For the sake of an apposite end-rhyme,
just here I'll call up a wind,

tired figure for inspiration,
for whatever good it will do.
Trite theme—initiation,
the wide world blood can show.

The wind keeps cantering toward us,
so the quarry's deaf to our coming.
Later life looms before us,
or so for now I am claiming.

I should add that this is the solstice,
a very short day in the year.
How apt for Amory Harris
and me. How grim, how austere.

Whether those pheasants in fact
are slaughtered or fly doesn't matter.
I'll say that our pastorale cracks.
The steadying past, with a clatter,

crashes to the ground, and we stand,
in a single moment diminished,
aware of our smallness, but *men*.
And now, before I finish:

my apologies, Amory Harris
(though in fact I've changed both of your names),
for dragging you into this chorus
of post-lapsarian pain.

These days, as an adult, you prosper, I hear,
you're respected, content, so they say.
Amory, I haven't seen you for years.
I've managed to keep it that way.

Reckoning

Let us not take it for granted that life
exists more fully in what is commonly thought
big than in what is commonly thought small.
—Virginia Woolf, "The Common Reader"

Once, on the steps of a cabin in wild Montana,
just before dawn I stood stunned
by a delirium of stars.
I've looked from a friend's apartment in New York
at nine o'clock in the evening,
likewise astounded by countless windows.
Light everywhere. Light everywhere. And dark.

Coleridge opined that the sublime
can make us feel like nothing.
I'm sure I'd have known as much without him.
The longer I live the less I aim
at grandiose observation.
It's best, I think, as I didn't always,
to keep my counsel in face of sights and themes

that lie beyond my ken, right where they've lain
lifelong, though once ambition
obscured all that. But I check myself:

I'm no more nothing, in fact, than anybody.
My memory feels boundless,
and if it fetches no sublime,
still moments may be fashioned into stories.

As randomly as I might choose a star
or a single light from some high-rise,
I summon a time—or it summons me—
when I walked with my daughter, then just three years old,
through a nearby patch of woods
to spy on a hidden beaver pond.
I longed for this adventure to unfold

exactly as it did. The wind came right,
and just enough of day
remained for both of us to see
three beavers swimming, a mere five feet from where
we crouched in pondside reeds.
Clear to this very day in my mind,
the hubbub of roost-bound crows, thick August air,

that tannic orange of the cruising rodents' teeth.
My daughter appeared enchanted
as we left the place by early starlight.

"How was it?" asked her mother back at home.
"Oh, Mom! You should have seen!
"There were some bugs in the water! They all were swimming!
"All of them were swimming around and *around!*"

In my early thirties, I didn't know
how not to feel let down.
I know some things today, that is,
that compensate for slackened aspiration.
That child's over forty now,
her children all older than she was then.
I study my daughter. I'm lost in speculation:

I resembled her, I hope, in intending kindness.
In my case, however, vague zeal
distracted my heart and mind and soul.
She's taking her own daughter to ski this afternoon.
They'll command an epic view,
yet it may be only the shape of a mogul
or cloud that, come the evening, the child will retain.

And my daughter? Perhaps by this time she has traveled
like me to where all types of light are local.

No Way Out

I reflect on days when I wandered from trash-clogged alley
to stylish parlor, politely—that is, inwardly—
crying out, *I want! I want! I want!*
I still smell perfume…Or was it sweat, and if so,
whose? I can hear rebuffs and even taunts,
perhaps the less pondered by me, the better. Memory:
realm of the unexpected, the coincidental.
I was ravenous for love, for the meaningful smile
I'd take as its token. Am I ashamed or wistful?
Memory guards what's holy. Or boring. Or vile.

One morning I put myself at mortal risk
by ripping open the door of that flaming DeSoto
(yes, it happened that long ago), accordioned
when the driver plowed at 40 into a pole.
Shocked imbecilic, she struggled to stay in the ruin.
I can see blanched knuckles on her hands as she grappled the wheel.
She wanted to save the clothes in her oversized suitcase.
Such beautiful things, she cried. *So beautiful, beautiful!*
I yanked her out at last. Still raving, she clawed me,
and to the end, I think, remained resentful—

I couldn't tell, or I can't remember, really.
Memory's fluid. Diluting my efforts at reason,

it's both a place of enchantment and of dullness,
and I look all through it as if I were keen of vision,
though I'm more than likely blind. I was a witness,
for further instance, to that glow on the other side
of a stubble field one evening. What could it be,
that shimmer? It drew me despite my nebulous fear,
and I felt near-disembodied walking toward it.
Can I fetch back a motive for being there?

It's vexing, but no. It's vexing, but no, I can't.
How damnably messy, recollection's redactions!
The aura? Nothing more than a pile of leaves,
set afire by that small-town cop when his shift was done.
He'd raked them down to the foot of his gravel drive.
What disillusionment, yes, yet it couldn't annul
that out-of-body sensation, though it had sprung
from giddy misprision. The scene persists, tart scent
of smoke and the blinking crystals of fall's first frost
in the dead-grass ditch of that skinny lane's dead end.

I swept up a new-hatched duckling before it was caught
by the roving fox that had killed the hen and murdered
her other young. There seems a rescue theme
in my thoughts. But what have I truly saved? That duckling

trailed me like a puppy, and I could dream
no greater delight than his trusting companionship.
When I whistled, he'd hustle right to my side, a wonder.
If only that were the story's close I could make,
before the neighborhood bully ran him over.
He claimed he never saw him from his bike.

A lie. Yet a motif of accident does emerge.
Will I make an effort here to account for that?
I won't. How could I, really? Of course I won't.
The duck had no escape from a villain's urge.
If I had an artist's gift, I could easily paint
that runnel of blood dried brown on the buckled asphalt,
with dots of down like meaningless punctuation.
How graphically to this day I picture it all.
The duck had no way out, as I have none
from the random and baffling incursions of recall.

II. Assumptions and Cullings

My Body Remembers a Day

My body remembers a day   that flavor on the tongue
a bit like a copper penny
there's the scent of lilies that pervaded the church's dank stone
no clock nor even calendar
has a thing to do with it I say   but I'm wrong

I know that's so when I study
how every year on the same late winter day
I'm reminded by my own body
whose cunning sends *memento mori* my way
as it did   good lord almighty—

back fifty-five years   one less than you got to stand
on earth before your own flesh
turned on you father and you went down   here I am
who by now have outlived you so long
my body almost believes we'll prevail in the end

and we'll forever remain
right here though that body aches   but even in those days
when I rarely felt any pain
except for some fight or hockey collision or fall
even back then there were signs

the odor   the taste   the pressure behind the eyes
these enigmatic prompts
a man can adapt to anything you'd say
including life in a war zone
whose hardships you carefully left unknown to me

for reasons I'm sure were compelling
you were right   one becomes inured   so I pay little mind
to the tale my body tells
I don't listen   that is I don't until I do
when my stoical effort stalls

and I find myself wishing the heart physicians had known
what they knew by 2016
when a pathway got clogged as it entered my own
old heart and in they went
I'm here as you would surely also have been

for years if only the doctors
could have done the things they did to save me
I wonder if another
sort of doctor might tell me why on the day
that marks your toppling over

my body delivers these cues and I almost believe
this mortal flesh may stay
in a place where time has no sway   no   and I'll be
beside you again and you'll hold me
I'm your child   and I'll catch a whiff of that oddly sweet

unlikely bouquet of sweat and bay rum and beer
I'll be safe as houses   yes   I'll always be here

2019

Some are apt to swoon over nature,
loving what they call harmony.
But Tennyson got it right on whoever
Trusted God was love indeed
And love Creation's final law,
saying *Nature, red in tooth and claw*
With ravine, shriek'd against his creed.

The gulls that once patrolled the Bay
of Naples, for instance, long since shifted
attention toward the city's landfill,
where pigeons, slurred as flying rats,
seek detritus like vegetable remnants,
fish bones, fruit stones, clots of sauce.
They're a bit like gulls themselves at that—

at least like gulls in ages past.
Now, in search of greater substance,
the seabirds have largely turned from refuse
and gathered rather in teams to maul
those pigeons. Not that gulls have teeth,
and not that we can rightly refer
to their blood-stained, webby feet as claws,

but you catch my meaning. The plunderers smash
their quarry senseless, then like so many
lions or hyenas, devour each carcass.
Is that what's meant by harmony?
Our nation's governed by a knave and fool.
Unnatural, you say? What's new?
The raptor gorges on its prey.

Free Couch

I can brood on things, such as why it's always the poor
who fashion slapdash signs saying *Free,* then stack
their detritus outdoors.

Who'd want it? I wonder, as I pass a certain house.
I know the people who live in there. Hell no—
I don't know them, not in the least.

There's some mystery in everyone, of course,
but souls like these seem somehow even more
inscrutable and dense

than their dismal dwellings. We make our grim surmises
about their behavior, mutter terse greetings, perhaps,
at the store, where they empty their pockets

to buy up futile tickets—Megabucks,
Powerball, whatever—Slim Jims and beer.
What do I bring to all this?

Is it sorrow, contempt, compassion? All these, to be sure,
and more, no doubt. As I drive by this backcountry place,
in whose mud-and-gravel yard

slumps a couch the color of their mixed-breed, brindle dogs.
Graceless scribbles bleed on a cardboard placard
in rain, but I see that, yes,

it's *Free,* this hunk of fabric and particle board,
which even the dispossessed elect to reject.
Drenched by ruthless downpour,

the couch sparks my customary inclination
to conjure up metaphor. But I keep myself
from making the thing an emblem

of perfect despair, because, whatever disorder
of spirit that sofa stands for, whatever kind
of psychological clutter—

is it really theirs, not mine?

Then and Now

A couple named Brown used to live together
in a house now deserted—on which more later.
I'll try here to focus on wider concerns:
for one grim example, the television's
report on two parents who've kept their children
shackled lifelong in darkness and squalor,

each sexually harmed, as I hardly need mention.
I've always railed against execution,
and yet for a spell I'm unsure of that zeal.
The oldest child is 25.
I'm briefly with so-called primitive tribes
who exact cruel public retributions.

Meanwhile, a leader exempts himself
from conflict of interest. It's his belief
that so long as he sits as president,
there's scarcely a law that applies to him.
Immodest, and worse. It should raise an alarm,
and in truth I'm often beside myself

over him and his lackeys. However, today
I keep recalling the Browns, Glen and Faye,
who lived just uphill. Their heirloom lilacs

must bear up this evening under sleet of late winter.
Will Syria go on erupting forever?
Like as not. But my mind keeps reverting, say,

to Faye, who appeared persistently bent
to her garden, now a shrinking dent
in cold earth. We all suffer from lack of proportion,
though I know I should speak for myself alone.
Hawaiian security, some time ago,
broadcast fake news of missiles sent

from North Korea, causing widespread terror.
The president heard of this quite a while after.
Thank fortune, I think. He's impulsive enough,
who knows how rash his response might have been?
My wife and I have granddaughters and -sons:
I should rally behind impeachment efforts,

but here's Glen again, as always genial,
smiling my way from his tractor's saddle.
I know fraught global events are transpiring,
I know I should tend to such goings-on,
but I need to clear slush from our front steps soon.
And I constantly conjure Faye in her straddle

of a row in that garden, stooping over
like one of Millet's hard-laboring gleaners.
She glances at me, for an instant straightens,
then waves a gloved hand, which trails a nettle.
Love never fails, says a famous epistle.
I grit my teeth not to hate certain sinners,

though I know I'm bound to fall far short.
I inwardly see the rotting supports
of the greenhouse the Browns left behind years ago.
Those two were so stalwart, so modest and sane.
Wind shivers a slat on the old structure's frame.
It now seems a godsend: the Browns lived next door.

Irruption

At dawn today, the fog still slept on the river.
The sun of a seemingly endless, Hadean heat wave
had not yet broken through, so I drove to the launch
for a paddle. Green herons, smart as sentries, patrolled
one bank. A beaver sculled beside me, blasé,
for a full forty yards, peeled branches bright in its mouth.

I thought of Emily Dickinson's famous claim:
> *Several of Nature's People*
> *I know, and they know me*
> *I feel for them a transport*
> *Of Cordiality*

She lulls us dull with such sentimentality,

so that as the poem concludes her chilled reaction
on coming across a snake—well, it strikes like a snake.
I tried to focus on Cordiality.
Aware of my own delusion, I willed myself
to ignore an intrepid kingbird's pursuit of an eagle,
bully who may have succeeded in robbing her nest,

and I looked away from the cove where last summer a doe
showed floating intestines, coyotes having ripped her

just as she made her leap for salvation by water.
I stifled such things this morning, my strokes narcotic,
my breathing steady, little else coming to mind.
Back at the landing, as I walked to get my truck,

I noticed a tree frog pathetically hopping across
the launch lot's pavement, out of its proper surroundings.
I stooped to carry the thing to mist-moist grass,
then suddenly saw that this was one among hundreds.
An irruption, in fact. Now what could have brought them up
from safety under their daytime earthen shelters?

If I tried to fetch my boat with the truck I'd crush
countless of Emily's "people," no way around them.
So although I felt tired, I righteously carried my kayak
across that little distance and hefted it up
to the rack on my roof and secured it, bow and stern.
When I heard the unmistakable crunch of tires,

I saw what racks me tonight: four stubbled men
in their own truck, towing a monster boat.
Through closed windows, I heard them, rowdy with booze already.
And here I sit, hours later, a man ashamed

he did nothing to head off inconspicuous slaughter.
No, I jumped behind my wheel and sped for home,
where I write this, feeling zero at the bone.

Politics, 2023

The long-haired cat in my rearview mirror,
flat on the tarmac—was it racing
for a freedom it would never know?
Did it flee a coddled life?
Not much I pass would suggest as much:

double-wides—two with Dixie flags—
pastel-sided like cheap Florida motels,
appear somehow to glare at each other
across minuscule yards full of kids' toys.
Everything's muddied by rain.

This latest shower darkens the coats
of three ribby ponies. I wonder:
do they ever get ridden? They vacantly gaze
over paddock wire, but at a distance.
They have their reasons:

yellow insulators suffice
to remind them electric shock
will greet a touch. They all seem well beyond
any penchant to fight their fate. The eyes
of a tethered pit bull glitter: he'd like to get at them.

Now I cruise through town. The dead axe factory,
empty storefronts, Dollar General.
For some reason, a few men shriek
at a sopping few on the opposite sidewalk.
One man, who doesn't look lame, keeps shaking a cane.

I don't know a thing. I keep going.
I'm a lucky man.
I get along with most people I know,
who get along with most *they* know.
Some of us have treasured friendships for ages.

Feigning unconcern
—though why would those strangers care about *me?*—
I sing along with country tunes
on a radio station. So easy to harmonize.
The same three chords every song.

Checkout

Just as some self-styled seer
might claim to interpret a litter of tea leaves,
I presume to read a life
by what this old fellow lifts from his cart.
How dare I? And yet I do.
Dorito chips dyed a strange orange hue;
a six-pack of Angry Orchard,
hard cider cans that bear the image
of someone his age, but scowling.
It doesn't bear any resemblance at all
to the zesty liquid that stood
in wooden barrels in Jersey-filled barns,
back when farms here were small.

Now he's unloading a little tin
of so-called Vienna sausage,
at one time known for whatever reason
as "log-haulers," somehow favored
by woodland teamsters who deftly drove
their strapping Belgians on skid roads.
I get a sudden odor, unpleasant,
that seeps from the waffled garment
that shows through an inch-long rent below
his flannel shirt's frayed collar.

Not the whiff of timber or cattle. The shirt
is so worn it shows nothing a person
could rightly specify as a color.

This is the lane with the sign,
14 Articles or Fewer.
He seems reduced to fewer.
Canned beets; a box of powdered doughnuts;
grape jelly; instant pudding.
I wonder what earthly blending
of these might make anyone's meal?
I cradle the weight of the grass-fed beef
I'll soon lay down on the belt.
It's a heavy weight. Blood stains the paper.
Who hammered the steer to its knees?
Abattoir workers must work to sustain
their apathy through the slaughter.

A folded cardboard shim will fit
under a leg of the table
so as to keep it more or less steady
on his trailer's canted floor.
What show is that on the antique TV?
I don't know. Neither does he.

No photographs in view. He builds
a pyramid of cans
by his plate. If ever there were children,
they're gone; likewise his wife.
The rail-thin girl at the checkout counter,
diplomatic, clears her throat.
When I look up, he's left.

How did he walk, I wonder?

Suppose I were an unremarkable

            bird, a junco, say
(I do like juncoes), couched beneath
            a brush-and-sapling canopy

at the edge of a patch-cut. Then I could simply
            be a part of late winter.
Now and then I'd dart out, my tail-spot
            flaring and disappearing. Right after—

back to the scrub. There are times when I long
            for such hiddenness and shelter,
for few to pause and notice me
            as they passed by. Of course, I'd *be* there,

but they'd feel scant interest in my look or my voice.
            I'm just another human,
but there is—what?—some *conspicuousness*
            in me, some loudness. Or so I imagine

in any case. If my bones were hollow,
            if I were flimsily clad
in feathers, I could be less than any
            x that marks a spot on a map.

Of course this yen for modesty
                    is absurd, not to mention vain.
Why should I think that I'm widely regarded
                    or that anyone cares about what I say?

Yet I'd like to hide lest something I've done
                    bring me shame or dishonor.
If I've sinned, I can't say how. Perhaps
                    I'd as soon not hear an answer.

And so in daydream I cloak myself
                    in a slate-colored garment, and talk
with a voice that few would stop to hear
                    on an ordinary walk.

Partners and Pardners

In the pre-op room, my wife was given
a scalene block for a *brief procedure.*
She had shoulder surgery three months back,

and now again they'll anesthetize her
to break up scars that have kept her in pain.
She'll be comatose, however briefly.

I remembered right off how one's love can seldom
appear so precious as on a gurney.
I feel what I felt on watching her labor

to give birth to our children; but I won't be on hand
for this episode. I sit in the lobby,
alone except for one other old man

in a black cowboy hat, who's waiting like me
for a wife to come to. He plunges his fingers
into her purse, and digs around

inside—in search of what, I wonder?
I can't decode his half-audible mumbles
or his face's expression. On the trip here from home

we hit black ice on a busy road
in this busy small town. My pickup spun
on the slick in what passes for rush hour here.

The fact we weren't hurt defies all reason.
Like grace. The man keeps probing, and I—
I keep wondering why. His look's still deadpan.

I know very well what it is to divert
one's thoughts from hurtful or frightening matters,
to seek what can lift us out of the world

when it threatens to tear itself to tatters.
How on earth can love torture us so?
Its pain seems deepened by the length of its years.

An ambulance siren winds down outside.
I've been reading to keep myself busy but now
I look up to find my cowpoke in tears.

Assumptions and Cullings

I sometimes come upon headstones in backwoods graveyards
circled by shallow depressions the size of bathtubs
and by brush, through which each one juts valiantly upward.
Lately, whenever I take to my local river,

small cavities in either side's sand tiers
look empty to me as those graves must be by now.
Once there were hundreds on hundreds of bank swallows there,
darting jauntily out of those minuscule lairs

to harvest the mayflies that rose from the silty streambed
toward the sun, like bright diminutive angels.
Now I feel lucky—a word too poor for what's sacred—
to behold one or two of the birds, athletic, winged

wonders under dawn- or twilit skies.
Assumptions scattered, the world a mass of cullings.
One tradition tells us our spirits will rise,
before which, however, a winnowing's required.

How odd to imagine that such an idea might comfort.
The men and women beneath those knife-thin stones,
the vanished wildfowl—to me, of course, pure strangers.

Yet I feel haunted by aerial things. They hover

over my frail boat as I remember and mourn.

What We Know, Who We Are

I call the brain a maze   so trite
        no matter that it's so
and describing it as a bad neighborhood likewise
        but in fact that's what we know

so okay I won't go there without somebody
        okay sure okay
sure it's full of figurative buried bodies
        which nobody can deny

I could claim that in that shadowy room
        normal looks unfamiliar
that those shadows are cast by a hangman's moon
        o have at it   poetaster

and imagine the path to it fringed by iris
        sure I can say whatever
insist it's not just a lair of sadness
        but of all sorts of hopes and hungers

still now and then I long to escape
        and visit a far-off star
don't all of us have kindred hopes
        isn't that who we are

Overdose

He spoke of how one day he tried to find
distraction by cleaning out his attic.
As though he could. Up there he came upon
his son's toy Tonka tractor, pocked by rust.
It seemed a relic from an ancient age
but something too the boy might use right then.
As though he could. "That was *my* overdose,"
he said, but smiled, then told me how it felt
as hard to look away from that plaything

as to lift great weights the way he could do
long years ago. He kept on lowering
the toy's bucket loader then lifting it,
like digging something up. And he knew what.
"I can just imagine." So I told him.
As though I could. His son wore one earring.
It sat in a dish on the mantelpiece.
He said, "Go figure. It doesn't crush me
the way that stinking yellow tractor does."

Once his son fell from drugs, he claimed, things came
to him as metaphors so stale he wished
that he could crush them all. As though he could.
Rainfall, nightfall, dead leaves that fall each fall,

rivers falling into awful ocean.

"On and on," he sighed. My response was slight
as the year's first flakes, which barely covered
the ground as they fell. I repeated it:
"I can just imagine." As though I could.

III. The Rural Sublime

Omen

Loud wingbeats at the window
snap me out of the torpor
of my minor springtime sorrow.

A blast of desire, not wholly
carnal, not wholly not,
suddenly overcomes me:

I'm almost 80—and lovestruck.
What can that have to do
with a cardinal's frenzied attack

on his likeness there in the pane?
Bright bird, I see that you're jealous—
of what? You're at it again,

enraged. Small wonder you're scarlet.
Listen: you're only alone.
Aloneness. Somehow I feel it.

A futile bird-brain ardor
brings on a premonition.
My love's in the bedroom, dear reader,

and I picture my world's perdition.

The Rural Sublime

Farmwives conjure elaborate quilts.
Woodworkers busy themselves at their stations.
No shortage of craftspeople here, to be sure,
but however deft these artisans,
their work's no balm for my sudden unease.
Today I've sampled maple balls
and *poutine*, and from provisory bleachers,
heard the roars of the Tractor Pull,
and outside of airplanes I couldn't see,
the gunmetal clouds dropping ever downward.

I'm at the Tunbridge World's Fair,
set in a hamlet from picture postcards.
I've been awed by oxen with legs so long
and stout that if my eyes didn't wander
to mammoth heads (we're all so small)
I'd imagine black-and-white trunks of trees—
the Holsteins—and winey red—the Herefords.
There's a scattering too of paler breeds
like Brahman or Charolais. All wonders.

Wonders everywhere in fact:
80-pound Hubbard squashes and pumpkins,
Brobdingnagian potbelly hogs—

"Kevin Bacon," "Spamela Anderson,"
"Tyrone the Terrible"—that plod through the final
Pig Race, intent on the cookie reward.
Though I feel the weather grow ever grimmer,
the announcer rattles his comic words
at the crowd, consisting mostly of parents
with enthusiastic sons and daughters.

Is any gripped by nameless fears
like me? I shuddered less when leaning
from a Ferris Wheel car or in the wild orbits
of the Tilt-a-Whirl and Whizzer Demon
than standing right here. Pink cotton candy
cones look like torches, puny beacons
in a rapidly dying afternoon.
The ozone scent of imminent lightning
fills the air like the whiff of corn dogs,
funnel cake, hush puppies frying.

During Pandemic

A green tractor roams that field. Who on earth is doing
winter farm work, and what on earth can it be?
I've parked for a spell beside the Connecticut River
just to look at the world. A giant rooster-tail
of snow behind the machine, which oddly matches
the color of its exhaust. Small snow at that
for late in January. The river's ice,
swept clear by wind, invites cliché: *like glass.*

It's as though the spray off those wheels and those diesel fumes
and the overhead clouds were conspiring in further cliché:
evanescence. I ache for something fresher
as I ache for May, the fields gone green as that tractor
and thronged with migrant snow geese. They'll resemble
their eponymous snow. I'll blink away the illusion
of drifts. A friend I loved for fifty years
expired two springs ago, a man so dear

I'm sad even now—and uneasy. Which of us isn't
edgy and blue in these times? I'm enchanted in marriage,
but my age would suggest I can't be that much longer.
And there are children too and children's children
whom I'll be obliged to leave. Above the thrum

of my sinfully idling engine, I hear the train
that makes one trip upriver and back per day.

The freight is even slower than the tractor,
tracks not what they were when along this valley
the timber trade was thriving. Now I'll stop
such useless, sorry reflection. If I don't, the train
and tractor and field and geese not yet arrived
and struggling farm—they'll all be metaphors
for ephemerality, and the theme's too worn.

It would crowd out any other. Needless to say,
my trials derive from merely being present,
but all of us are that. No, not the gone ones,
but I'm not yet among them. I wipe the windshield,
fogged by my breathing. It *was* only breathing, no?
The tractor's gone. The sun has blasted through.
Where does it come from, this thought as I pull away?
It was once just right for bombers, this clear sky.

Shadows

—*in mem. my brother Mahlon*

The shade our tamarack throws
grows paler every day,
just as its needles do.
Odd, an evergreen that's not.
How can you be forty years dead?
Each last needle will soon have fallen.
I look up from writing this,
and it's muddled, my perception,
as though I had some something
in my eyes, almost
like a needle too.

Those eyes, against my will, go blurry.
Again. The rain's a subtle drum
on every tree in the forest,
but I focus on the one.
I've gotten so fond of it.
It's stood apart for most of my life.
Four decades the world's been without you now.
That single tree is spilling itself
on the ground. In mind, the shadow
of its canopy will live on

even after it's gone.

I Arrive at the Scene

All of a sudden, a crowd,
most of us pretty much strangers,
which seems to me—well, strange:
our village and others here
in this stretch of valley are tiny.
But Howard, who's been the chief
of the volunteer fire department
for years, shows up exactly
as the ambulance crew appears.

I do know Howard. We live
at the same end of town. He's quiet
and decent. He sees what we've seen:
blood on gravel leading
to a woman tangled in weeds.
Roof-down, that's her old crate
in the brook. There's a gallon of milk
in a bottle, standing up
on the tar. The glass didn't break.
A miracle. I've heard

someone say about our town,
it's a place where all of us fight
and all of us love our neighbor.

71

Everything in her sack
was strewed or squashed or smashed,
except the jug of milk,
which she bought at a neighborhood dairy,
and that's why it's in glass,
not a grocery store container,

the waxy kind. One man
thinks the woman came to his church
a time or two, then stopped.
The EMTs do something
to her skull with a sort of sleeve
made out of metal and cloth
before they load her up.
Can anyone say where she lives,
or lived? Howard shoots me a look,

not good. She might have done better
if she were made of glass.
I know that's stupid. I'm thinking
a bunch of ridiculous jabber,
but I'm also thinking about
my family, how bad things happen

not just to bad people. Of course,
that lady *is* a stranger—

so good or bad? Who knows?
I want to be asleep
or learning to play the piano
or oiling the .32-.20
my uncle left to me,
though it's not deer season. Besides,
I don't hunt them in my late years.
I wish I'd been doing something
that wouldn't have let me arrive
in the first place at what's before me.

Whatever I did, it would suit me.

Fall

—*Washington County, Maine*

I make myself ignore the limb-perched osprey
and the mink that nimbly slithers cross-stream.
They're commonplace, routine.

I'll focus instead on October red in that maple.
But what is *red,* after all? Is it crimson?
Cochineal? Scarlet? Carmine?

Is it *r* at the very western reach of the spectrum,
most distant kin of this overhead *v*?
Maybe something like bloodshed or ruby?

The color remains beyond my capacity
to depict, like a being immense, transcendent.
I won't argue about its existence.

Choiceless, I'll affirm, at least for the moment
the inescapable hopelessness
of all I might seek to express.

For now, let that insufficiency be praised.
The fall will take all this away
—I mean all that *all* might be.

There's no need for me to talk out my reveries,
I think: Observe. Revere. Adore.
Poetry, vexing chore,

feels as naked as next month's trees.

Upcountry Detour

An old man sluggishly waves a hand.
He looks spellbound, as if by an apparition:
A stranger, me, in a place few visit.
I'm sidetracked into my own odd spell—
Both sadness at bleakness and fascination.
There's a sign in another dooryard, bizarre:
Atrini, World's Finest Files.

A softball arcs on the blistered common,
A father pitching, a son at bat.
One newer car, a Dodge Charger, glitters
Like gemstone in front of a postage-stamp store.
Back lots full of witchgrass show unwheeled pickups
Dead amid whips of lilac and sumac.
I drive out of town past further signs:

BECKYS TRUCKERS HEAVEN ONE MILE
COME IN AND HAVE A "CUP" WITH BECK
BECKYS CLOSED FOR RENOVATION
Its windows, boarded over with wanes,
In brush beside it, a bedspring, a dryer.
I notice a black cat eyeing a bird
On its roof, too high for him to consider.

76

Violence

—4 August, 2023

We once longed to have our eagles back.
And back they came, from poisons that doomed
so many over the years. At last,

they're common again. This morning, I saw
two wrangle over a hatchling loon
in the crown of a pine. Their little war

shivered the boughs like earthquake. I figured
one had carried the prey to that tree.
I tried to look away. I didn't,

but watched till they ripped apart the chick.
Each raptor took its portion away.
Entrails hung from the larger one's grip

like snakes I've seen in such terrible talons.
Our crackly portable radio brings
a retrospect of the monstrous explosion

in Beirut, four years ago precisely:
reports of the dead, the homeless, the maimed.
Tritely, I think, however you slice it,

I want the whole damned world to change.

At the Apple Shack

—6 November, 2018

As winter's icy winds lope south,
I stop at the apple shack,
not far from here, just across the river.
The place will be closing soon,

in fact, next weekend, the one before Thanksgiving.
I'll stock up for the holiday.
We all, especially the grandchildren, cherish
Honey Crisp, Macoun.

Stick season now. The hills have doffed
their radiant garb, gone subtle.
It's all dun and yellow on oaks and beeches
that vainly cling to dear life.

Our oldest son is 50!
This sprawling house, come the holiday,
will be in cozy disorder,
full of treasured quirks:

one toddler, for instance, likes to wield
our long-handled metal shoehorn,
which for unknown reasons he calls a *voter.*
For him it seems a weapon:

he'll charge around the living room,
voter brandished on high.
Aptly, this is election day.
In the ballot booth, I said prayers,

unorthodox, for the troubled nation,
for some decency, for a silence
of weapons, for love to prevail, as it will,
thanks be to love, when we're gathered.

As I pay, I tell the orchard's owner
how much we all will miss her,
how we will miss her fabulous apples,
though the time till her shack reopens

feels shorter every year.

Winterberry

Almost perverse to slide the canoe
onto Little River in late October.
Wet wind rushed sideways and brought a scent
I'd soon enough come to think of as boding
snow once my winter senses came back.

Often you do things simply because
you always did. So it was that day
last fall. I had no mission—that is,
none I knew until I knew it.
Five mallards flushed from reeds with a clatter,

but the ducks weren't it—whatever *it* proved.
I envisioned the bed of coals that once winked
through the plates of mica in my woodstove's door—
woodstove I used when I was young
and efficiency didn't concern me whatever:

to put up ten cords felt like recreation.
Be still and know that I am God
is a passage from Psalm 46 I've cherished.
But the current didn't want me still,
and the scurrying clouds didn't want that either.

So I thought, in my lust to posit design,
and to find myself at its very center.
I shrugged such a vanity away,
for the river as ever was just a river,
the clouds remained no more than clouds,

and I still only I. And yet,
having skirted an eddy that formed at a bend,
I drifted onto a flat that—wonder!—
appeared to be altogether unruffled,
and all around me on either shore

and stretching clear to the bordering alders,
stood bush after bush of winterberry,
for whose sheen the word *red* feels simply impoverished,
its radiance all the more striking because
of the gray into which I had launched, unwitting.

The Flowering of the Farmer's Widow, 1958

All sag and ache and fourscore years of second-guesses,
she plucked the last black rooster for stew. The Belgian gelding
nodded in clouds of pollen blown from pines. At least
the blackflies didn't come into the house, whose wallboards glimmered
at night with phosphor.

> This couldn't be grief. So what *was* she feeling?

It wasn't as though she'd forgotten his yellowed knobs of tooth
as they ripped at bacon, his rough wide hands, the ear-splitting howls
and contrariness of his damned Plott hounds—which she put down.
She'd never have to chase that horse again to pen him.
He hobbled near

> then shied when she snapped her kitchen towel.

The stable flies had gnawed a nasty welt that shone
like a bright new penny on the Belgian's withers. He had one claim
to grace, her husband: his eye for color. *A bright new penny...*
That sounded like him. He was mumbling something about the purple
in a raven's wing

> just as the wind dropped that limb on him.

She'd been watching. His brother took forever to dig the hole
among back-lot rocks, her husband too cheap to buy a spot
in the marble orchard. She'd get one now. She wouldn't lie out

in a field with him, all muck and dung. The granite chips
had flown off that brother's pick.

        They glinted, pretty as frost.

She buried him with his pure-gold watch. She didn't want to.
But for every loss, some gain: she soon would sell the body
of the horse for glue and dog-meat. Let people call her the Devil!
In her mind, the butcher's big sledge fell, the beast's blood flared,
flowed into a gutter—

        in her mind, which had bloomed at last, at eighty.

A Return to His Senses

My mouth was full of that metal taste. There were purple brackets on
    my vision.
My legs weren't willing to swing from bed. As ever, I believed my
    dejection would be
never-ending. And yet it ended, as ever.

So I walked to the boathouse through a northwest wind, which
    striped the lake with foam,
as if late July were September. I thought I saw spume passing eye-
    high, but of course that
was imagination. The scent of bacon rushed in from somebody's
    kitchen, a whiff of a
wood fire somewhere, water as clean as anyone's heaven.

I picked a hard little blueberry.
The gloss-green skin resisted my bite.
The sudden tartness struck me as somehow perfect.
I felt the minor burst, and small contractions inside my cheeks.
Though such a bird wouldn't normally cry so in such a blow,
a loon delivered her heart-heavy wail.
Upwind from where I stood, it was something I could hear—or
    maybe feel.

The white door bellied at my push, groaned across the damp-swollen
     floor.
Cobwebs clung to my brow.
My eyes blinked only a moment, adjusting to gloom until it wasn't gloom.
Blond paddles hung on a wall, and no one to fashion them now.
Good Earl was gone, who made the best ones, claimed my late father.
Things came to mind at that: I forced them back—as I did that father.

I'd take the longest paddle and slide out onto the surface.
I'd pull against the waves for what I was worth by God to gather a mile.
I'd notice the flex of the slender shaft's fine ash.

The canoe was of canvas, and green, and likewise fine.

From under the sunken sill, all golden spangle, swam a yellow perch.
It settled in lambent troughs of sunlight on the cove's sand bottom.

I'd pull like a strong young man, which was how I felt, untired.
Then I'd turn, bow high in the spray, and ride the bright waves back.
I would not need to by now, but I'd drop heart-heaviness overboard.

I'd drown it down in the deep of the lake.

IV. Stories of the Fall

Until We Do

This morning just after dawn
a fox crossed in front of our house
against the snow he looked perfect
as Dürer's paragon
I dream that I'll see him in mind
forever   we don't speak of death
we don't until we do

November First

Forlorn. It's as though the word had been there lurking
within the calendar's paper,
waiting for me to turn October over.

In the instant, I hear a perfect interior version—
as played by Bill Evans, who wrote it—of "Waltz for Debby."
Paul Motian brushes his snare,

subtle, near silent. That pair
of opening, falling fifths spawns melancholy
all by itself. I really ought to refrain

from admitting cliché to the page:
how my youthful flamboyance long since surrendered to age;
how my years have made me patriarch of our clan;

how the oaks' mahogany leaves have replaced their naked
neighbor maples' verve;
and the usual rest. But platitude's what it deserves,

such facile dejection from one who should count himself favored,
nearing the end of a life that numberless souls
would crave, so much of it seeming

happy accident. Things might have been
so different in any season in my little world.
How dare I so much as imagine desolation?

A chickadee cheeps in the forest.
However implausibly, I can make something of it.
The bird's no nightingale, and still I'll hail him,

as ever grandiose, bookishly clever:
Forlorn! The very word is like a bell
To toll me back from thee to my sole self!

And yet there's so much more than self to consider:
Debby, *musa incognita*, for instance,
performing her waltz, heedless of my existence.

Mere Humans

Tink shouted, "Did you hear my bad news?" I turned
from bucking up firewood and killed the engine.
How different he looked, our tough old bantam
neighbor—a rascal, but stolid as stone.

Here stood a suddenly tinier version.
No one in town would believe he'd cry.
Things had to be bad. He told me why:
"Mike's gone. Some business called...*aneurism*."

I caught my breath. Mike? His grandson?
Dead before forty. Tink and Polly
had practically raised him up from a schoolboy.
(There were troubles with the in-between generation).

Tink's gone, but I see him back twenty years,
red oak sawdust pooled at his feet.
I still can't believe he actually weeps.
Two-stroke exhaust smoke loiters on air,

although yes, I've choked the saw dead quiet.
Mosquitoes strafe us. And now I recall
Mike passing in front of our house last fall,
trailed by the 6-point buck he's shot.

Two flecks of blood have dried on one cheek,
and in spite of November's chill, he sweats
from dragging that whitetail out of our woods.
For years he's been bigger than Grandpa Tink.

So is the deer. (Mike will give our family
good venison backstrap later this autumn.)
Who'd predict I'll go over to Tink and hug him?
Not even I. It's surprising he lets me.

How long does he soak my shoulder like this?
Long enough, it seems, for me to sense
something like splendor in this awkward clench
by which I'll always feel shocked and blessed.

Innocence and Experience

First warm spring day. A melody
pours from someone's window.
Unlike me, the player is young:
notes stutter from that piano,
the music more moving for that, of course.
The child's youth hurtles away

at daunting speed, which the player won't sense
until a later day.
Up through thick foliage of village trees,
plink plink plink.
The tune is one whose author and name
I used to know—I think.

My Mother's Bedjacket

Its color soothed me. It might have been called,
if not quite rightly, rosy.
Nothing has matched it since I was small.

The fabric must have been something like velvet.
It felt more than merely soft.
Since those days, in fact, I've touched nothing like it.

The pillow she used in unsettling darkness
as she lay by her gentle husband
shared the smell of that supple garment.

Was its fragrance artificial or rather
the scent of a lovely young woman
before years and liquor conspired to take her?

It seems I still ache for that old aroma.
It hasn't been replicated,
will never be. How did I climb over

the four-poster's rails, or did she lift me?
I hope she lifted me.
I've resolved the sorrowful rage that eddied

between us two for too long a time.
I forgive her: after all,
I had a part in every storm.

With a coarsened will, for decades—well after
that father died and left me
broken—I fought to turn my mother

back to what she could be no more.
I cursed her stomach-churning
breath as I hauled her up from the floor,

as I tried to scream away her roughness,
to shout her red face back to pink:
all futile, given her whiskey-deafness.

But still this longing, however faint,
to climb and lay me down
near that nameless hue and odor and scent.

November Elegy

—In mem. S. E .A.

We were on your coast—Point Reyes.
Some people had kindled a bonfire on the sand.
We paused to look. Late autumn here in the east.
She seems oddly brave,
                    Venus, off to my west.

I watch the scenery fade.
Near dark, there's a ribbon of woodsmoke over the trees
and the scent of it reminds me, however obliquely,
of that beach out there.
                    Can two years have passed so quickly?   .

By the ocean, we hummed a song
as we'd done together at someone or other's picnic
decades before, the first time we met: "When a Man
Loves a Woman." We'd started
                    at the very same phrase, in unison.

That synchronicity—
a wonder. It meant somehow we'd be friends ever after.
Again I feel it—sorrow's familiar stab.
I knew the things
                    I could count on to make you laugh

and weep. I'll accept my grief.
I can't do otherwise. Now something stirs
the leaves. The leaves are dead. Only memory stays.
A northerly wind
          has hustled the smoke away.

Stories of the Fall at Eldercare

His collapse may not have produced a thud, though later
there'd be several witnesses who swore it did.
We're easily seduced by our own narratives:
the truth, to call it that, can quickly become
no more than a concept. Those who heard him fall,
or assert as much at least, were there at PT.
The therapist didn't turn around, she supposes,
because the sound of his topple had been so subtle.
At that very moment, she claims she was demonstrating
a stretch that eases pain in the lower back,
and as she did, she faced away from the group.

What, I think, if there *was* an audible thud?
Maybe the therapist needs a story herself
to justify her slowness to respond.
She says he crumpled back at the rear of the room,
which likewise might account for her not hearing,
despite the fact that several men and women
insist they started shouting right away.
The therapist concedes this may be true,
but reminds us that what might well feel like shouts
to aged folks can be whisper-quiet to others.

More than a dozen souls in that small space,
including the leader, which means a dozen stories—
no, even more. I look down onto the river
from the small café in which I sit drinking coffee
with my friend, the firstborn child of the elder who dropped
to the carpeted floor, with or without a noise.
Nothing quick would have saved him anyhow,
he concedes, it seems without rancor. *But now the State
will send their inspectors here to poke around.*
Yes, I muse. Then they'll contrive a list

of so-called facts. For me just now, the facts
are these: the water looks as flat as a mirror;
a distant mountain is standing on end within it,
swathed in the muted red of April buds
spread across its flanks below the tree line.
So beauty prevails, a truth that's oddly linked
to the grief, however prosaic, I see on the face
of my tablemate, who mutters, *It was coming
sometime anyhow,* then resumes his silence.
Perhaps he's formulating the tale he'll tell

to his own three children about what happened to grandpa.

Maturity

Yawning, he greets the day as he does each morning.
His coffee pot runs on a timer,
two slices of plain white bread go into the toaster,
an egg drops into a pan.
He extracts a deadhead tulip from a hallway vase.
He's come to believe
in the salutary effect of regular habits.

Better to nurture routine
than…he stops. That throb in his skull's more electric
than painful. He means to ignore it.
He takes up a knife his mother once gave him for Christmas,
ideal for the grapefruit before him.
His ennui has value, all right. He could easily draw blood.
He touches the blade to a knuckle,

perhaps to prove to himself that he hasn't lost
inquisitiveness entirely.
He used to insist complacency was a sign
of failure. His orange juice glass
shows beads of condensation. There's a shimmer of heat
above the toaster. Beyond it,
the view's as familiar to him as his signature.

His constraints are self-imposed,
though who'd have predicted the way his life would turn out?
He recalls himself ranting for justice,
but there's just so much you can do in a single lifespan.
Perhaps, if she were alive,
his mother would say he should have *applied himself.*
She always did. Now his pleasures

are mundane: a timeworn armchair, mystery novels,
square meals. He's tried to forget
the hero who'd fix the world as well as the singer
who'd rock the house every night.
He prefers his house unrocked as he ages. It is.
In his head that strange pulsation
persists. He admits it's mildly distracted him,

though he tells himself it's all—
well, all in his head. He's selectively reminiscent:
he used to run rapids, say,
in angry rivers. But that was years ago.
On his plate, the wedges of fruit,
with their pink, symmetrical shapes, invite his attention.
He surprises himself on finding

he still holds the same sharp knife with its age-browned blade.
He ponders that knuckle again,
which looks like a small white onion there on his hand.
He pricks the skin that sheathes it—
with delicacy, not force. He watches a globe
of crimson shimmer and glow
like a tiny Christmas tree bulb. Its light is the light

that sifts through a dusty window.
What of that droplet? He thinks, *Let it suffice.*

Old Leather Suitcase and Me: A Fable

I found this suitcase slumped in a dark attic corner
like a drunk awash in self-pity. *I* was *Me* once.
There's a burn mark beside one latch. I tell myself,
with a bit of wonder, *Me used to smoke in those days.*
Indeed—and drink. And booze and bright ash equaled char,
perhaps in some airport waiting area. I see
such moments, as when Me stumbled out of that bar,

precisely to catch a plane. On the way, he kicked
a sack that a woman had stuffed with gift-wrapped somethings.
Her look mixed fury with fear. She wore a toque,
dark green, with a sort of oval metal badge.
So much is blacked out, but the hat is clear for some reason.
Me mumbled *Sorry.* The grip's travel tags have frayed:
Hungary, Italy, Switzerland, even Egypt!

Me held fellowships, took exotic vacations
with his wife and their children. A raving child himself,
Me knew even then he didn't deserve good family.
I bring to mind his foot-stomping rage in Siena
when a toy he'd bought wouldn't work on his son's fourth birthday.
Although Me reassured the child that his rage
was not at him, the boy's face was more than just worried.

And when the shopkeeper claimed the toy had been dropped,
Me re-erupted, screaming until frail knickknacks
quaked on the small store's shelves: *Non sono bugiardo*
neanche truffatore! I'm neither liar
nor crook! Maybe not. But brute? No doubt. Or yes,
a brat mid-tantrum. The shopkeeper, quaking herself,
gave Me the refund: in fact, the refund-plus.

The cobbled Sienese square was generous with sun—
and looked to Me as dark as the hell to which
he must be bound. He was poet and scholar,
whose Italian stay had been funded by rich foundations.
He hadn't yet turned up his cards and found his hand
to be worse than a simple loser's. All this before
Me met a man he hasn't seen since then.

Me, his hope grown faint, felt mostly puzzled
when the stranger, unbidden, recited this passage in English:
I will destroy the wisdom of the wise;
The intelligence of the intelligent I will frustrate.
Me inwardly cursed the stranger for his presumption,
for playing the saint. Yet the passage lodged inside.
The bag obliquely recalls that old quotation.

Back then a person's luggage had no wheels.
Back then, full of books, this suitcase felt like an anvil
on walks to airplane counters. In Budapest,
it got lost for a week, and Me was well spared to know
no Magyar to speak of. What might he have screamed about this?
Now Me has grown old. He is I. These are not the sole reasons
these days I'm not very apt to raise my fists

as Me once did, nor to storm at innocent people.
Never in those bad years had Me been aware
he knew so little. What he used to consider acumen
had brought him to where he ended. If I've found a shred
of wisdom since, it has come of ascertaining
my own unwisdom. I study the scorch on the suitcase.
It has prompted a story, I see. May Me keep hiding.

Zach's Mystery, and Others

We remember Zach's hating himself so much toward the end
he became a walking—no, a stumbling cartoon:
he left his apartment, say, to look for a brick,
not some handier thing like a lamp or a frying pan,
not just any rock—he left, and found his brick
and used it to smash his grubby bathroom mirror.
Cartoon Bible-thumpers would likely have shouted,
The end is near. Dirt-poverty, that was one thing,

the lack of beauty in life was quite another,
and people turning away wherever he went,
the ones still willing to hear him sore as hell
they remained so. And something else: he couldn't count
the years that had passed since somebody called him *dear*
or whatever. Well, I guess that's a *lot* of things.
Those Bible folk I imagined would have been right
if they'd meant the end of Zach's pathetic world.

We remember how we'd drink with him, and more
than half our gang are dead as he is now.
But some of us gathered those thousands of little shards
and managed to fit them together again like puzzles,
and so we all had mirrors that we could inspect
without thinking of bricks or drinking. But we kept thinking—

not all-day-every-day but plenty—of Zach,
of how we were like him and how for sure we weren't heroes.

We just woke up one day and we were alive
and it wasn't because we were smarter or God knows better
to look at than Zach. (And I say *God,* by the way,
because what the hell else do I have for explanation?)
Before it all shattered, Zach had a movie star's features
and smile, an athlete's body…I could keep listing.
Not beauty or brains or courage—none of that saved us.
But we did get saved and Zach and some others didn't.

Standard Time

*...skateboarding's values have always appealed to those
who consider themselves somewhat outside of society's pace.*

—GQ

We just got a photograph of a grandson, cherubic, at the local skate
    park.
His smile shows he's pleased to have been adopted by the older so-
    called thrashers,
though he hasn't yet learned like them to be tough as nails, or to
    look that way.
I'm not sure why I think of Buster,

except that *his* toughness is real. He too looks incongruously cherubic,
though I wouldn't tell him that, and if I did, he might not know
what I meant. He also might not like my explanation, and then
I'd wish I had somewhere else to go,

and quickly. I passed him today. He was mowing a lawn. If he hadn't
    been,
he might have been digging a grave or tuning his pickup or maybe
    splitting
some wealthier neighbor's firewood for winter. I've never asked, of
    course,
but Buster—or so at least I'm guessing—

109

doesn't consider himself a rebel, though he did quit the highway
    department
ten days before he'd have been entitled to a pension. He was that
    pissed off
at his foreman's high-handed conduct. I'd call that genuine rebellion.
Buster's face is weather-buffed,

which lessens the cherub effect, I grant you. The kid to our
    grandson's right
has a skull tattoo on one arm, and barbed wire inked around his neck.
He shows a nasty expression. Whereas the brim of his hat points
    backward,
Buster's brim points dead ahead.

I notice the scowling, tattooed boarder is stripped to the waist,
    whereas Buster
as ever had on the shirt that laborers seem to wear all over:
collared, Army-surplus green, with blotches of sweat at his armpits
and on his back from shoulder to shoulder.

Buster, I think, embodies the meaning of what's called *eking out*.
When I passed him this afternoon, the light was dying, because it's
    November.
I know something better than I did at the age of those thrashers,

half-naked and surly,
let alone of my grandson—or even Buster:

the cold comes on at a pace nobody can keep outside of forever,
and the darkness shows up early.

The Widower: 24 Hours

He wakes as usual and pushes himself
To routine: to instant coffee, bacon,
Toast, the news. He eats at the counter.
He dusts the front-step rail for no reason,

Then pays the bills, which are smaller, fewer.
Pausing to look through a window, he seeks
Patterns among the cars and trucks
That defy the effort: they teem like insects.

They bear commuters and other cargoes—
Food, drugs, trash, the papers.
The two young marrieds next-door call up.
When he visits, they suggest meditation.

"We never knew ourselves before,"
They claim. He loathes their herbal tea,
But he sips it. They're sweet. Great canyons crack
Between himself and their histories.

Absurd, or some related term:
That's how one older friend will choose
To lament with his wife their decision last night
To invite him for supper, given his moods.

Or so he imagines, and who could blame them?
They both got up and left now and then
For the kitchen, meaning to *check on something*.
Their words were fuzzed by an oven fan.

The three sat down to passable wine,
Salad, potatoes, beans, a roast.
He picked at the food. Somewhat later, he pissed
Into their toilet, darkly, eyes closed

Against trifling signs of their common lives:
Her glamorless bras and his boxer shorts
On a drying rack in the corner. No,
It wasn't some bed of roses, and yet…

Tomorrow, he'll rise for his daily shower.
Those towels with the *His*-and-*Hers* monograms:
Packed away long since. He'll fix himself
A meager breakfast and eat while he stands.

Disappearances

Rapt, an old man inspects his living room mirror
but not for his image. Instead, its angle
subtly reflects the light of a stub of candle
on the silent piano. He might say the reflection *shimmers*
but the years, though blessed, have jaded him some.

He'd rather avoid such a hackneyed word
but he's also abandoned the urge to think up a better.
A train comes to mind, though he doesn't know why.
He can't recall when it was he saw it or even
if, but it seems some caboose's lantern

lodged in his mind a lifetime ago, its glow
growing distant. Was it even then a matter
of things he longed for fading? The rattle and click
on the tracks make a poignant song. He'd rather
ignore its meaning, clearer now than ever.

Oak

Why all the wind these days up north where we live?
Our round little mountains used to keep it smothered,
but this roar of air just now is enough

to make our sweet dog tremble, who tends to reserve
her fear for thunder. I confess I also shudder.
One looming oak, smooth-clad in green,

slaps back the sun up there on the hill, its stance
triumphant over the gale, while weaker trees
salaam in abject obeisance.

Birches and poplars look daunted. You needn't remind me
I lend them features peculiar to conscious beings.
Yes, I project what I feel upon them,

though I know I'm the conscious one. I'm full of blood
not sap. And I'm scarcely calm before dire warnings,
lacking the courage I impute to the oak,

exemplary courage that I will never attain.
All manner of violence—poll-axe, saw, or sleet—
may cleave the oak. Still it remains

staunch to the heart. Our woodstove's losing heat.
I drop in logs, a couple from lesser oaks.
In spite of the sun, I anticipate pain.

I'm only one of the wide world's frightened folks.

Via Negativa

He beholds a ragged windrow of snow,
dull remnant, and wonders if drink or dope
might not kiss him and make him better.
The writer knows they wouldn't, couldn't,
or hopes he knows it, hopes he'll recall
the gloom and sometimes utter madness
he left in his wake, for him and all.
The windrow is dun, tarnished by duff.
He sits benumbed at midday, no matter
that in this place, far north, at last
the hillsides' modest display has come,
primed to explode once April is over

into all the hues that neither he
nor anyone else will ever depict.
That palette will always defy mere words.
He hears two men—Bill Frisell, Jim Hall—
whose guitars play "I'll Remember April."
Yes, he concludes, to speak is encroachment,
while the music sounds eloquent, masterful.
But even if power of speech sufficed,
Who would care, he wonders, *and why?*
The writer knows he must marshal patience,

mindful that something always comes.
Or better perhaps, nothing does. Yesterday,

those same musicians half-broke his heart,
but uncannily—though the matter's familiar,
of course, to any lover of art—
at the same that they reassured.
What's wrong today? he asks this noon,
as if the question were something new
and an answer something he'd find on his own.
He has used his usual tricks, compiled
a list of people, for one example,
he ought to be thankful for. It was easy
to make it lengthy. Yet here he perches,
jaw set, prepared for life to crumble,

to go to pieces, as in fact it hasn't
for decades now. (Beyond the music,
he hears glass breaking; voices blare.)
He feels such an urge to make things *mean*,
including his mood. He's had that longing,
drunk or sober, all his life.
Outside, ungainly flakes start falling
that seem to resemble mica or talc—

unsnowy stuff at least. They stipple
the field. The guitarists' tune has stopped.
Volition will put each white dot out,
the way one might a row of candles,

erase the gray-brown drift of snow
he considered only instants ago,
abolish the few inchoate leaves,
and make that raven with a twig in its bill
dissolve in sky, as it does. Or rather,
his God, or call It what you will,
can darken every light until
what he conceives as his spirit breaks,
as it did so often years ago,
and then, thank God, it broke forever—
or so in his addledness he fancied.
It was there that his life could start all over.

Stay broken, he mutters. *Life can start over.*

Small Thanksgivings

Without these hearing aids,
I'm deaf as a clod of dirt.
I wouldn't deceive a soul
about that. As if I could.
And after a certain age,
vanity's only for fools.

Without the hearing aids,
I sit on our porch in mid-spring
as peepers chant by the pond
—or so I'd have to be told:
absent these little gizmos,
I don't hear their music. There's none.

Nor birds'. Nor noontime church bells'
just half a mile downhill.
If I don't wear the hearing aids,
I wander around unheeding.
My wife must exercise calm,
I so often mishear what she's said.

One day she asked, for instance,
if we should eat chicken or chili
for dinner. *Who's cross-eyed Shirley?*

I asked. She simply chuckled.
She indulges her husband, retired
some years ago. If he weren't,

God knows what he'd do, his alarm clock
quiet as the old saw's mouse.
But the world's manifold sounds
have returned, praise technology.
I was moved to reckon my good fortune
by a scene I happened upon

last week in our tiny airport,
where a bored, solitary woman
from the TSA must wonder
if excitement will show up one day.
But when an aged deaf guy
set off the security buzzer,

she knew right away, of course,
this wasn't excitement. Just age.
She patted him down and felt
some foil-wrapped pills in his pocket.
She took his metal cane,
laid it with care on the belt,

guided him gently through.
On the farther side, he waited
for his wife, whose face was a study
in impatience, even rage.
When he reached for her hand, she snapped,
"Don't hold me! I told you! *Don't hold me!*"

He stood there unhearing, palm up.
I sat outdoors with my wife
last night. The peepers were busy.
I was all ears as the sky
went satin and stars prepared
to show. This woman still strikes me

as a study in beauty and grace.
After more than 40 years,
my wonder at that hasn't lessened.
Last night, holding hands as dark fell,
in silence the two of us listened.
In gratitude we listened

to frog-song that could well have been
some exquisite recital of woodwinds.

For My Wife at 67

Autumn at hand, I recollect how you combed every wisp
of weed from your garden in a pair of separate Septembers, each one
for a different child's
wedding here. Though the mess came back too soon—

pigweed, purslane, vetch—I'll never forget how you knelt
in the scrabbled dirt; how you smiled; how the muddy, sweaty droplets
coursed your face.
The bald faced hornets had hung their nasty basket

again on our woodshed's eaves. Uphill in their thicket, red squirrels
would assemble to raid the feeder the minute you filled it with seed
for pine siskin and junco.
I was thinking of winter, you see, even though what I heard

from the porch was only the somnolent hum around that hive.
You'd rap the kitchen window, the squirrels would take to their trees,
then scoot right back.
The afternoons would have shortened. Things repeat.

Whatever could have happened that such bounty fell on me?
Whether I'm with you or not in the flesh, I adore you daily.
And luck keeps on coming.
You've been my path to sanity since you were 30.

Yes, things have repeated through our many years, though we've known
occasions when nuisance alone seemed to rule, when I pondered how
our raptest attentions
must come to nothing. But I look at you just now,

and then I appraise myself, that less-than-hero who won
the shining girl. That only happens in movies.
A marvel a day,
a single marvel—that's surely enough to hold me.

Alone at 79

Unhungry, he cracks a single egg.
Were she not away,
the two of them would as ever applaud
its yolk's deep orange,
scoff at the pallor of store-bought.

Now he blandly notes some color.
Were she right here,
they'd praise their good fortune
at their little village's having
a minuscule bank with a cheery teller,

who raises free-range hens
and sells the eggs with bold yolks.
He ought to feel joy at all of this.
The one daily train groans down the valley.
Eight hours will bring it back up.

There's a certain way his wife
can cock her hip. It stirs him,
as does the familiar scent of her skin
when she comes in from cold like today's.
She won't come in today.

He's planted himself in the kitchen rocker.
What does a mere egg's lucency do
against that one plate in the sink?
In his older age, retired, self-indulgence
means leaving the toilet seats up.

She'll call this evening. The day gapes.
They hiked the lower Alps
on their honeymoon forty years back.
This morning, he briefly brightened
to discharge small chores.

He fed the usual chickadees
and stoked the woodstove, not once but twice,
and washed that plate, though it wasn't dirty.
She's gone away
for another full week.

When they both were young,
her *rs* were childlike. He loved that.
He beholds the splendent shadows
stretched long on snow
by a vivid late-winter sun.

Hardwood buds grow red on the ridges.
They do that each year of course.
He puts his elbows on the table,
his fingers to his temples,
his weeping unheard but by him alone.

A Late Moment

supernal—adjective mainly literary relating to the sky
or the heavens; celestial. • of exceptional quality or
extent: *he is the supernal poet of our age supernal erudition.*

The sky showed gray with the prospect of rain.
The poet thought himself anything but
a wise man, only one running errands.

He'd been somehow pondering his family's move
from a hamlet whose every dirt byway he knew
to one in which he started all over.

30 years gone. Now a sudden sun
flamed up on the dingy plow-drifts of March.
He watched three robins fossick in gravel.

These oddments reminded him of coming
for the very first time on this shortcut from drugstore
to grocery, a route well known to all

who'd lived mere months in this neighborhood.
He recalled how such small discovery
felt revelatory. By now he'd driven

the lane for decades, but like that sun
it broke on him: *I'm here!* Well, of course,
he thought with a smile, unseen except

by him, we all must always be somewhere.
Many, he knew, rejoice in good luck—
maybe not at unpredicted luster

on remnant snow, but, say, at the glow
on a church in Québec, or clouds that crowd
the Serengeti, green sky in the Seychelles…

He stopped himself from going on.
But *supernal:* yes, it seemed wondrous and strange
that just then, of all earth's numberless places,

the one where he happened to dwell should prove
his own as his lucky years ran down.
But indeed it was—and so much of it new.

Scarlet/Indigo

> *. . . strength in what remains. . .*
> —Intimations of Immortality

By the pond, a maple
reddens already,
in middle August.
Impossible:
it still should be summer.
Fall's upon us,

most of the grandchildren
back at their schools,
moved up a year.
And the nation…
My great gloom blends
with more everyday fears—

five falls gone,
my heart had a clot;
I'm all right, but Steve,
dear friend,
is buried—cancer.
A good deal to grieve.

Much endures, it's true,
and yet it's hard
not to sense the shadow,
as the old do.
Here at the edge
of our late-shorn meadow,

small baubles shine:
five blackberries strung,
more dark than just blue,
on canes
gone leafless. The berries
should have vanished by now.

Brush bends in a breeze
that contains a slight chill.
Though tiny and poor,
it's sweet,
the fruit, even more so
than when I found more.

A Poet's Indolence

—on our anniversary

The sun having stooped behind the ridge to the west,
the moths come forth: Rosy Maple, American Copper, Ambiguous.
The remnant glow backlights each one on the screen of the porch,
where, in the warmer months, the couple takes meals.

Slowly, their galaxy will reveal itself, ineffably.
He might be restless, but for these moments ease prevails.
He might be refining words. It's what he does.
In earliest spring, he'd look for better, say, than *melting*,

and winter hardwoods would surely deserve better than *naked*.
In summer, he'd need to assign to green frogs more than *twang*
from the five-acre marsh a few hundred yards to the north,
and bullfrog song would certainly transcend mere *croaking*.

Yes, all of them warrant more, but not on his account.
Not now. The forecast calls for storms tomorrow,
and they'll have their splendors no doubt. Perhaps he'll go hiking.
For now, it feels better to sit in silence with his life's companion,

watching those delicate wings refract the ebbing day.

Blessed

So much migration soon:
the northern harrier flitting
like a moth along the verge of our pond;
the rasping grackles; phoebes;
adult loons lifting off the lakes,
their young ones to follow; geese, of course.
All away to the south or the coast.
We plan to stay here, whatever the season.
Hard to believe, my dear longtime mate—

mid-80s on the thermometer—
we'll need blankets before you know it.
And once winter's here, we'll dream of summer,
as one can crave day after dark,
or youth in senescence. A game that's absurd.
Yes, yes, but we both miss the sound
of our children's peaceful breathing, for instance,
in their bedrooms back when they were small.
Yes, yes, time flies by like birds.

Celerity, fleetness, speed;
movement, flux, mutation.
Name them what you will, they'll be
what they were and are forever.

133

How changed are *we* from what we've been?
Who can say? Yet, blessed, we'll stay
as long as we can. We sit here in sun
as, earlier every day, it dies.
We hold on while the planet spins.

Mythology

That I had to stay out of the pond for half an hour
after I ate. That my grandmother selflessly rolled
dressings for Yanks who'd been wounded in World War Two,
that her uniform hung in our parents' cedar closet
but somehow disappeared. Perhaps there were thugs
in masks who grabbed it and lammed. Oh sure. I invented
my own little myth as a boy six decades back:

that if I thought hard about her in the shower,
a girl would appear by magic and she'd adore me,
the spray from the head the very ichor of Eros.
It never happened. I never thought hard enough,
perhaps, or couldn't picture which girl I wanted.
Which has changed. That whoever threw the first punch in a fight
would always win. I have scars to disprove that claim.

That marriage went dull, its physical fervors quashed
by the passage of time. It depends on whom you are paired with,
I'd testify: I wear two wedding rings,
the first for day one, the other for fifteen years,
and I'll soon need another for forty. If this is a trap,
don't set me free. Such sentiment was hardly
the point, if indeed there was one, when I began.

Ah, well. *All's well,* said the fabulous Bard, *that ends well.*
As I've found—like a wondrous myth, like a fairy tale.

Compensation: The Apple-Pickers

—in mem. Elizabeth K. Jordan

As ever, she steadied the paper
with her left hand, the right one wielding a nub
of charcoal. This time she worked on a sketch
for what would become her painting
of eleventh-hour apple-pickers—no, later,
too late. But she wanted November:

frost on grass, ghost-white,
fragile as silence, against which her figures
would be stationed, the pillow of leaves below
the tree: umber, gray,
subtle shades she rightly considered a challenge.
Everything challenged her,

Because, and she likely knew it,
the brute fact was, she painted poorly.
And thus, her grandchildren all believed it
a marvel, after the sketch
gave way to canvas and oils, that the picture proved brilliant,
as if it were crossed by magic.

It implied unseen things: for instance,
crows, which showed nowhere in what she produced,
could still be heard, nearby and raucous,
outside the frame. And we caught

the scent of windfall fruit. Or rather *I* did,
as I never told my siblings

for fear of being taunted.
All of us loved her—and laughed at her too.
We'd spy on her as she studied the easel
on her sunporch, biting her lip,
shaking her head, then dabbing again at the palette,
lost in thought, no doubt.

May our laughter be forgiven.
We were ignorant, not callous.
Like her, if only once in our lifetimes,
may we be gifted with something
that transports us beyond mere chronological measure,
as she was by her one good painting,

which compensated her
for ongoing griefs: losing a son
to the flu epidemic, and then soon after
losing her husband. *The Apple-Pickers*
seems to have been her stingy Muse's gift
not just for her valor, but for her persistence,

for simply putting in time.

Affirmation

We saw the wound in the woodshed's sheathing,
which soon explained the midnight sound
that had snapped the two of us out of sleeping.
Our old dog bayed like a horror film hound.

A chipmunk or squirrel had made a hole
for winter behind a tier of wood
we hadn't burned, and to wait out the cold,
had filled it with seed. So there I stood,

in barnyard boots and underdrawers,
to untangle the tale. Her den-time past,
a bear had ripped away three boards
and rifled the rodent's paltry cache.

There were her tracks. Who would have thought?
Compared to the unpredictable stories
nature provides, the ones we concoct
prove for the most part ordinary.

So plain a perception gave me pause.
Laying my lust for invention aside,
I studied the gash the bear had clawed.
She allowed me, so long as I squinted my eyes,

to turn the ruin into a flower,
an orange-rimmed set of petals arrayed
around their dark interiors. Now—
would such indulgence last a day?—

I granted the bear the easy judgment
I'd offer a child, who, perhaps knowing better,
defies the civilized world's proscriptions,
making off with something she considers

essential to sustenance—or pleasure.

Suspension

Season of the Strawberry Moon, the Algonquins call it.
The berries ripen in June.
We see them along what's left of ancient tote roads.
Some say Rose Moon, some say Hot.

We won't be, but if we were forced to forage,
those shy red baubles wouldn't start to stifle our hunger.

If solitude can be shared, we share it here
in our cabin, deep in the woods.
Don't ask where it is.

There are gullible perch in the lake.
Under damp duff in the forest, small worms for bait.
We own a stable rowboat.

Rain dripped all day from the eaves,
then blue broke through
exactly on time for moon to delete it.

Our crackly portable radio says: fair tomorrow,
hot but pleasant. More good fortune.
What did we do to deserve this?

In a jagged row at our clearing's edge, wild roses glow
like gemstones splayed on felt,
mere minutes before the darkness yields to moonlight too
and they go wan.

We noticed a damselfly drying its wings in late afternoon
on a wall beneath the eaves.
It lifted just at dusk to hover briefly
over its tiny world,

as we do over ours.

Animate Objects

i. **Duende: Last Day Out**

> *the mystery, the roots*
> *fastened in the mire,*
> *that we all know and*
> *all ignore.*
> —Federico García Lorca

I've come here after protracted contemplation
of a duck at home—a roughly fashioned decoy.
It has sat, unremarked, on its dusty shelf so long
I couldn't even recall where the fake bird came from.

And now, instead of hiking through March's mud,
boot-sucking, I've driven myself to this coffee shop,
The Local Buzz. There was never an apter name:
chatter, a bright percussion of spoons, and something…

My meditation, or whatever else you'd call it,
continued for minutes on end, though I scarcely noticed
I'd been watching the duck until at last I stopped.
I can draw no conclusions from that odd rumination,

yet something...I now know the decoy's swells and divots
as I never had, nor imagined doing before.
But surely something beyond such trifles held me.
How does a person pose throughout a lifetime

as something called a *poet,* and yet remain
bogged down in unknowing, as dense as one of those pastries,
soft and sticky under their glassy dome?
You may object that the simile is weak

and eccentric both. Why should I play, however,
at anything else? Why, when all I can offer
is *there must be something?* No matter: I sense a strangeness,
the chitchat seeming suddenly now to have vanished.

In the silence, something flows through this busy place
like a fathomless underground river, though I can't hear it.

ii. **Old Lenses**

For years they've been more decoration
than objects of actual use,
these old binoculars, couched
in their scuffed and torn leather holster,

each of its wounds, very likely,
an emblem of something. Who knows?
I plucked them out today,
mid-morning, our breakfast not urgent,
quarantine all over,

and we without obligation
I felt suddenly, oddly moved:
the binoculars were given
to my wife the day she turned twelve,

a time when she yearned, she has told me,
for a cowgirl's life, one somehow
epitomized by scooching
next to an open fire
to eat beans from a long-handled pan.

We have lived right here for years
in a bowl of round Yankee hills,
though at twelve I pictured the Yukon,
slain caribou dressed and smoked

and hung in a ramshackle shed.
Each of our dreams—so expansive!
With seven grandchildren between us,
all crucial parts of our joy,
we tend in actual fact

to hunker down anyhow,
our pain during quarantine
chiefly the young ones' absence
and that of other loved ones.

Fat flakes of late-season snow
are falling, taking their time
to settle and disappear.
No sun. The world all slate.
Only mourning doves on the ground

near the feeder, slate themselves
in such somber light. My eyes

have aged: however I tinker
with each of these dusty lenses,

what I see is blurred, and might be
a clump of dogies grazing,
despite the vast prairie's wind,
or a musk ox herd on the tundra,
circled as if to defend

from a not quite perceptible danger.

iii. **Nest**

Though we are more snug
than most besieged by the virus could rightly beg for,
still I wander around the house in search

of subject matter.
I have to do *something*, my soul perforce its own
society for protracted stretches.

My wife has concerns
as well. I haven't looked at the nest, half-lost
on a sill in a living room that's become

too big for two—
I haven't looked at the thing in years and years.
And even if I did so before,

I'm sure I shouldn't
refer to the act as looking. I believe that now.
That's what struck me as I stood there, humbled.

What else have I left
unnoticed? I balked at touching the structure

with a hand that might in a trice turn toxic

out in a world
growing more exotic with every hour. How wondrous
the weaving that made for what I observed:

grass and twig
and a shred of fabric. Whom did it clothe,
its blue fainter now than one of the eggs

that may have touched it?
Was the nest my love's? A friend's? A stranger's? A child's?
I, who have vainly prided myself

on my eye for nature—
I have trudged lifelong through nature's realm mole-blind.
I incline my ignorant face to inspect

a mere wisp of down
and a bit of shell, a shard about the size
of a baby's tooth: the last and only

sign of life in the making.

iv. Toy Boat

On my quarantine hike, I study some tracks sealed away
beneath the trail by an overnight scrim of ice.
I think of how for wildlife, both hunter and prey,
a day means a fight to endure. But then, of course,

no beast bemoans its life, which is merely its life.
But it can't of course be any of this that reminds me
of my fiery grandpa. I had just reached five when he died,
so I know what I do of him from family stories.

Perhaps it's that before I came out my eyes fell
on a little toy boat we keep by the tub for our grandkids.
I had one of those myself, one that I'd sail
around the old man's belly, which broke the surface

of his bath as he lathered and rinsed. He sang all the while,
and even I could hear his voice's beauty.
I considered those tales of his ire as I hiked up here.
What lay behind that ancestor's fabled fury?

His voice was famous, it seems, all over our region,
and young as I was, I could tell his songs were sad.

He'd married a belle, according to family legend.
Needless to say, he never could have foretold

that a horror like multiple sclerosis would plant her
—from early on, for good and all—in a wheelchair.
It must have floored him, but as for me, Grandmother
was chiefly the silent, white-haired woman who sat there,

spellbound, it seemed, by her tall blond radio.
I later would learn that she especially loved
Eddie Cantor's evening variety show.
Her husband wrote Cantor a letter, more funny stuff.

These were its words, complete: *Dear Mr. Cantor,*
Balls! Sincerely yours, Robert C. Lea.
Holding the note like a knife, my father said later,
my grandfather bolted off to post it upstreet.

Now I'm standing here, where a turkey clawed for acorns,
and where a hungry coyote missed it, if barely.
I make out the big bird's scrabble to get itself airborne,
up to a bare March limb. Below the oak tree,

the predator waited a while. It's all easy to read.
The turkey's not gloating. The brush wolf feels no wrath.
Failure is common when the world's wild creatures seek
whatever they need to survive. Grandpa collapsed

and died one night after chasing a streetcar driver
who'd failed to stop. He meant to attack him with fists,
no doubt. Yet even that death came in for laughter,
and the incident showed, some said, he always had grit.

After he'd gone, I'd frequently see his wife cry,
which both confused and filled me with something like terror.
Of course, back then at my oldest I was five,
so I had no means to decode adult behavior.

Compared, as I say, the animals' world seems simple.
It's famously there a matter of eat or be eaten:
these iced-in tracks I've found will do for example.
In my grandfather's case, I'm left with speculation.

I do recall it took time for me to circle
around that ample stomach with my little boat.

I suspect he never so much as sensed its ripples,
his songs so possessed him. The songs were lovely and gentle,

though I summon not words but sad sounds that rose from his throat.

v. **Carved Grouse**

By now I feel more amusement
than anything else at the sight of the oversized bird,
which bears a closer resemblance
to a Rhode Island Red than to any grouse I've seen.
One leg was half-dismembered
by one of my favorite dogs when he was a pup.
In summer it keeps a door
from swinging back and forth when a blow picks up.

And then there's that damned little plaque.
Somehow I prefer that I be called "Sydney"
in such instances as my name
is used in some context that might be construed as public.
At times my part seems vain
in trying to save the planet, but that effort's the reason
I have the fat bird, a gesture
of honor from a group well known for conservation.

"To Syd," the brass plaque reads.
Well, better than Jake, my brother, got on a pintail—
untrue to nature as mine—
from the same well-intentioned outfit when it honored *him*:

on his plaque, "Jack" is the name.
With the years, as I say, I've moved from mild displeasure
to a smile on seeing my grouse,
along with a subtle but lingering sadness over

the loss of the dog who gnawed it.
His registered name was different from what we called him:
"Fish Pond Storm" was "Pete."
I likely reminisce on our dogs more often
than a saner man would do.
If a family loves a dog, it should live as long
as all in the family itself.
I hear the winds of March. As in that old song,

they make my heart a dancer.
I try to repress the notion the winds are foreboding.
I have always kept the collars
with tags that name each vanished pet and pledge
to reward a lost one's finder.
Those collars are stored in a drawer, I think, although
for the moment I can't think which,
I open it so rarely, almost as loath

to look at them as at snapshots
of our sons and daughters back when they were small,
which instead of delighting bring me
wistfulness and sorrow. I try to retain
perspective, to know that really
Jack or *Syd* or *Pete,* even *duck* and *grouse*—
each and every name,
even of trifling objects around the house—

will ride away on the wind.

vi. Alien World

I'll consider the physical properties
before I muse, or my vague Muse does,
on what I might call ontologic.
I'll fail in both cases. There are two slim rods
of what looks like verdigrised copper
and a few strands of coarse black thread,
but the rest is made only of cow-horn—
the model ship, I mean, square-rigged:

hull from the portion nearest the skull,
yards from farther up,
proportions shrinking along the spars
to the yardarms, fashioned from the very tip.
The material features, come to think,
are in fact not many. So onward,
little else to do with our world
closed down. The boat was my wife's late mother's.

She was lovely. I wish she were here.
But she's gone, and the schooner's provenance with her.
Now I'll consider the breed of the beast.
I know cattle, and so am trying to figure

if it's Scottish Highland or Texas Longhorn.
You see, the vessel is wrought
from a single horn, and those are the only
cows I can conjure with length enough.

My mother-in-law had exquisite taste,
though, schoolteacher that she remained,
she rarely had much cash at one time.
Her collecting, needless to say,
consisted for the most part of objects
from places she'd actually seen.
Texas, or some southwestern state?
To our knowledge, she'd never been,

and Highland cattle in her salad years
were still quite uncommon in the U.S.A.
I must contemplate such a meager enigma
since we seem, with the virus, locked here to stay.
My pent, petty fancy turns the ship
into a small Flying Dutchman boding
doom. No, perish the thought!
Better to heed, outdoors at evening,

the lyrical call of coyotes
above the thawing ice's racket,
and the barred owls' eight-note altos
and the lilting descant of a late-winter freshet.
And yet the mind falls back
to the mystery ship, which by now has cruised
the stony mantle over the hearth
for year upon year, as if unmoored.

vii. **Game Trail**

*Nel mezzo del cammin di
nostra vita mi ritrovai per
una selva oscura ché la
diritta via era smarrita...*
—Inferno, I

Day seven: was this midway?
For me, no question, it wasn't
the middle stage at all
of *la nostra vita,* but was it

midway through the plague?
Surely not, of course.
It's up to me now, however,
to carry on perforce

as if there were no such thing
as the virus—or an end to my life.
Which meant this morning I sought
the daily exercise

we're told will keep us sound
well past an idler's time.
Perhaps. The sun was devoured

by cloud come seven a.m.,

and so I considered some rounds
on my faithful indoor gear:
a stationary cycle,
a rowing machine, a bar

that sheds two bells each year.
After all, I won't get stronger;
but I mean at least to defer
getting feeble a little while longer.

Then despite cold rain, I set off
outside instead, resolutely.
But my thinking as ever ungoverned,
I recalled *I started Early*—

Took my Dog as I walked,
though Emily's trek was a rambling
by oceanside. Nonetheless,
mine had a feature resembling

her own: a vague sense of threat.
I noticed two spheres full of bones

and fur, a splash of white,
and a feather on the ground,

all dropped by an owl from a limb
of the beech I was leaning on.
I plucked up the feather and stuck it
through a hole in the battered crown

of the trail-worn ballcap I wore.
Was my odd fatigue a symptom?
It felt, at all events—novel.
A sudden, soul-chilling frisson

supervened, if only briefly.
No symptom, I reasoned—I,
who'd been housebound, so it seemed,
for weeks. I recognized

that the sudden shiver came,
precisely, from recognition:
a game trail lay before me,
freshly and heavily trodden,

and it was the very one
beside which I'd set up my stand
to shoot the very last whitetail
buck of my life. Since then,

I've somehow wanted no other.
The trail ran straight as a chain.
For the wildlife it clearly meant
la diritta via, The Way.

Some questions rushed in on me,
despite my resistance; they were
a fool's, but I entertained them,
even knowing them absurd:

was my sparing those experts on fear
a portent of how I would later
learn what I'm learning today?
However right my behavior,

a threat, as for them, may lurk—
undetected, but always nearby.

viii. **Through Our Kitchen Window**

the outside world provides for daily splendors,
weather allowing. Nature has its patterns: east, of course,
sun rising, west setting—and numberless others, though not as the
    sentimental
imagine. Harmony? Balance? Tell it to the squirrels, the gray ones, so
    rare here
till lately. But pattern, to be sure: bumper acorns in recent years
means many squirrels means food for bobcats means more of the
    cats than ever.

I had seen just two in the woods in my long life-time, and those
    mere flashes.
Car sightings were glimpses as well. This winter alone I've seen many
    more,
including the one that was backlit today by the morning's earliest rays.
It looked to be taking a casual stroll along our ridge. We felt the gift:
something out there we could link to the marvelous. The sun ignited
    its pelage
while it strode, then paused, as if to pose for our sakes—as of course
    it did not.

It's only that we yearn, like most these days, for signification, no matter
"false christs and false prophets arise and perform signs and wonders,
    so as to lead
astray..." And many just now believe such prophecy. Reason enough,
lies abounding from the empowered. Much depended on the
    animal's radiance.
How might I have felt if we had seen a stalk and a bloody attack?
I have small reason myself to attack certain types of fellow humans,

the ones whom, only moments ago, I sneered at as sentimental.

ix. **Old Walking Shoes**

The shoes seemed marvels to five sons and daughters,
and still they're here—as who'd have predicted?—
those toy plastic sneakers, bright blue, with a key
on the side to wind them. I remember the children's

eyes going wide on watching them start
to take their brisk steps, in some cases before
those children themselves could walk. I noticed
the shoes as I headed out the door

for my own walk on what we call The Loop,
old game beat sustained by our longtime back-
and forth. We know each inch: half a mile
or so from our house, there's the dull brass plaque,

benchmark by USGS on a headstone,
or so the pale rock once appeared to me.
Now, though I'm slow as eighty impends,
I've pledged to fend off such simile.

Next I'll find branches, shorn and dropped
from oak to trail when last winter loomed

by porcupines in their ardor for nuts.
Next comes the vernal pool, where soon

the boisterous gray frogs will start up their yatter,
and my wife will have to talk more than loud
if she wants her deaf husband to hear what she says.
Spring's sounds will return, no matter these clouds

and this sudden thrumming of snow mixed with rain.
Near the end stands the hill where once, at five,
our youngest was riding high on my back
when I slid and fell. That same good wife

returned right after with clippers to crop
the thorn-whip that came too close to taking
the small girl's eye. But I'd started these thoughts,
before tyrant memory's usual break-in,

with some little blue wind-up walking shoes.
Now they fascinate small children once more,
eyes keen to watch them trudge the floor,
though all the old feet can manage to do

after so many years is a step or two.

x. Drum Ice

Those enclosed and dwarfed by stone and steel
may not know what I mean when I say *drum ice.*
Picture a brook or river or lake that freezes,
and then the water beneath subsides—flows off

in the case of moving water. Still, its sheath
of ice stays whole, a hollow space beneath it
over earth or remnant water or another
layer of harder ice. Whenever this happens,

the result, precisely, is drum ice. Quarantined
by choice against the virus, my wife and I
would go insane if not for time outside—
though it's too rare—on rambles through the woods.

Once, alone, I crossed a stream and crashed
through to my knees, which scarcely made for crisis,
the waterway no more in fact than a gully,
and I far younger then than now, and fitter.

But just this morning, passing near that spot,
my memory retrieved the old event,

and, even more vividly, an adventure tale
I came upon in a journal of some kind

when still a half-grown boy. The story told
about some northern woodsman's falling through
a tier of ice and facing a wolverine,
which had fallen through upstream. I can't recall

just how the episode worked out, although
it must have been benignly: after all,
this *was* a magazine for kids like me.
In any case, I recollect the horror

I felt on the trapper's behalf. The animal
owned a place far down in my soul for years.
I'd long since memorized the other names
by which some people named him: *Carcajou,*

Skunk bear and *Quickhatch.* And I knew
how fearsome this great weasel proved, and fearless,
sometimes even tackling wolf or bear.
I imagined nothing worse than being bound

in confining space with such a ruthless menace.

But as an unreasonable old man now, I think
I'd almost prefer such panic to sitting here
—albeit with the love of my long life—

pent up within this shrinking house for hours,
fearing some menace more obscure, *corona*,
which may be lying close, unseen, while we
might fall into its ken at any time.

xi. **Balloon and Flowers**

—for Goran Simic

I dropped into sleep while reading a book of poems
by the Bosnian friend I write for here. They're brilliant,
full of red flowers and graves and wrenching accounts
of his homeland during the 90s. They lend some perspective

on our COVID-19 scourge, which I don't mean to downplay,
much less to discount the unforgivable part
in worsening it of our leader, jackass and villain.
Goran's a Serb, and his wife was a Muslim woman:

during the troubles, he really had nowhere to turn.
His poetry makes my guts knot; it's not a sort
you'd think of as soporific, but being so anxious
for three generations of family has made me restless

almost each night, and so of course I was tired.
I'd been sitting in my wife's dear grandfather's rocker,
handsome but sternly wooden. I still nodded off,
and when I came to, I noticed I had drooled

on my shirtfront, like any old fool might do; and yet

the sun of afternoon through the kitchen window
turned even the spot of spittle to something lovely.
Unlikely enough, and the next things to snare my attention

were a once-vivid mum in a glass and a reddish balloon
left from my wondrous partner's 64th birthday,
back before we knew what the world was in for—
though that contemptible leader had been forewarned.

Our grandchildren's eyes turned bright as my wife blew out candles,
the smaller kids batting balloons like that one up
into air...All that before some weeks unraveled
and people got sick, many died, and that balloon

and that flower, sole survivors, puckered and shrank
to half their old sizes and somehow looked so sad
that I went back—it makes no sense, I know—
to those agonizing poems of plunder and murder.

xii. **Faulty Burner**

The winds of winter don't blast through our nail holes.
No ice skims over the water dish
for the stiff old dog come sub-zero dawns
before I drop new logs on old coals.
Today's shelter—solid. Today's dog—rambunctious,
and needing more workout than I can offer,
no matter my daily outback adventures.
But all I can do in this respect,
or any, really, is make an effort.
We both burst with restive heat, though I
can puff out like our range's fitful burner.

The house is well set to make its way past
the pandemic. There's only that one small threat:
precisely, a stovetop burner, whose flame
for no reason will now and then suddenly die.
But our freezer's full, the power sound,
and there's even a propane generator
to see us through any electrical failure.
Two up-to-date woodstoves warm the house,
which—unlike the first I knew as a person

who might be rightly described as adult—
is more or less new, no fixer-upper.

I paused with the dog on a ridge this morning
while run-off snow ran riverward,
and I all but thought my tears would undo me:
I felt an ache to have a friend
standing right there as he has so often,
in cityscape or in woods like these.
Dear companion of fifty-odd years,
he's racked with cancer deep in his being,
and is as of now in end-of-life care.
Some strange sort of vertigo overtook me,
and unconscionably, self-pity and fear.

My body appeared to be suitably strong,
yet I frantically thought of all I would lose
if I should happen to drop right there—
of things and people I *will* at length lose.
It came upon me as a bodily chill,
no matter that spring was on its way.
Now I sip tea at the end of the day,
my self-absorption for the moment repressed,
warm and secure as I have any right

to be as my generation stalls.
Nonetheless I'll be sure to keep an eye

on that faulty burner, which, day or night,
can put itself out in no time at all.

xiii. Clock

My great grandfather's upright clock was wrought in a village
in Lehigh County, Pennsylvania by a local craftsman,
who may have been the old man's neighbor. But I shouldn't say *old*,
my ancestor not yet that at all.

Having shaped the body out of fine black walnut, the maker, or
    someone,
rendered the beaming face of a moon behind the hands.
Is it wrong of me not to have had its inner workings
restored to function? It's almost as though

I celebrate their silence. There's a plaque on the cabinet door,
"Made in Emmaus, 1874," but the artisan's name
has sunk into the brass and vanished, the world being rife
with metaphor and *memento mori*.

Or so I can muse in too-dark moods, being old now myself.
That fact in itself seems scarcely linked to what I think—
except that I think it: when Fats Domino died some years ago,
my dear friend Stephen telephoned.

We've always craved the music that crossed into the mainstream
in Fats's day. My friend's very ill. We reminisced,
each grateful the man arrived just in time to rescue us
when we were kids from the Boones and Nelsons.

I still hear my first 45: *We happy in my blue heav-awn."*
I also hear my poor hungover mother's protest:
"My God, what *is* that?"Well, what it wasn't, to her dismay,
was the old-time Tin Pan Alley version,

all roses and strings. May the woman's agonized soul be at rest.
Just now I drink the splendor of sunshine through my window.
Days like this, so chiseled and bright, bring fall to mind—
they're downright exquisite, and yet, of course,

it's spring I should think of now. Autumn means silence, not song.
My friend has cancer. The hills are still fall-bare, but lovely
and sharp as fine carved wood, and the moon sheds gorgeous light.
Why November, then, that clichéd omen of winter,

our eleventh hour—which I haven't yet let my old clock strike?

xiv. Talisman

That I may rise and stand, o'erthrow me, and bend
Your force to break, blow, burn, and make me new.
—John Donne

Far south of here, the hired man called them
beet birds, his notion being
that they came as the beets' first green did.

It would be facile, I think, this morning,
sleet gripping the broadleaves' earliest buds,
to make our first goldfinch a trope

for hope. A dull winter, it's been, for birds,
right enough, nothing flashy on a given day,
only the same chickadees

and pine siskins, not even many jays,
as a rule unwelcome, for spots
of color. Perhaps dullness should be

the trope, in fact, because it's not
just Covid-19 that threatens the world.
I've embraced some gratitude—

rubbish and heat overtaking us all—
that I entered that world when I did,
today's intellectual life

and its social being ones I'm glad
(when a *visit,* say, is some techno-session)
not to have lived with for long.

Can a *friend* really be a set of electrons,
can public discourse survive on contumely
and witlessness? The goldfinch,

a female, is described as having, precisely,
"dull yellow underparts."
In our sequestration, we trust

that this one is merely a start,
that in time we will not want
for bright males and subtle females both.

And they *will* arrive—unless they don't.
My favorites, cedar waxwings, say,
once clouded our pond summer-long,

then plucked the flowering crabapple tree
right through till snow. Now I'm all but amazed
to see a group of three.

Well, why not admit it? I'm at that age
when men and women have forever sneered
at the ever-worsening state

of their world and of its heirs'
plain decadence. I've tried to spit
in the eye of this pandemic.

Come dawn, I've made myself opt
for blitheness, no matter I'm aware
just now how much of this

has been mere act. So be it. There
sits the bird—look! Why shouldn't we cleave
to such cheering signs as we can?

Why not keep our poses alive? Agreed:
I reverse myself. For example,
I'll proclaim that the beet birds will swarm

in a bright assortment so ample
as to constitute what once was labeled
not a flock but a *charm.*

ACKNOWLEDGMENTS

I owe significant debts, though some of my benefactors may not even know just *how* significant, to Martha Rhodes (greatly), Ryan Murphy, Danny Lawless, Robert Nazarene, Fleda Brown, Stephen Bluestone, Fran Richey, Nancy Mitchell, Tony Whedon, Chard de Niord, Cleopatra Mathis, Michael Simms, Goran Simic, Marjan Strojan, Michael Dumanis, and Ron Slate. As my dedication indicates, I'll always feel gratitude to the late Stephen Arkin, soulmate and abundantly helpful critic for almost sixty years. I'm likewise grateful to the following periodicals, in which most of these poems appeared: *Agni, The American Journal of Poetry, Artful Dodge, The Atlantic Monthly, Autumn Sky, The Beloit Poetry Journal, The Bennington Review, Brilliant Corners, The Christian Century, The Gettysburg Review, The Hollins Critic, The Hudson Review, Image, JAMA (The Journal of the American Medical Association), Juxtaprose, New England Review, Notre Dame Review, On the Seawall, Pleiades, Plume, Pratik, Salmagundi, The Southern Review, Sow's Ear, Tar River Poetry Journal, upstreet,* and *Vox Populi.*

And here are some answers to my title's question, *What Shines?* All my children and grandchildren and Robin, my life's companion.

A former Pulitzer finalist and winner of the Poets' Prize, Sydney Lea served as founding editor of *New England Review* and was Vermont's Poet Laureate from 2011 to 2015. He is the author of twenty-three books: a novel, five volumes of personal and three of critical essays, and fourteen poetry collections, most recently *Here* (Four Way Books, NYC, 2019). In 2021, he was presented with his home state of Vermont's most prestigious artist's distinction: the Governor's Award for Excellence in the Arts.

PUBLICATION OF THIS BOOK WAS MADE POSSIBLE BY
GRANTS AND DONATIONS.
WE ARE ALSO GRATEFUL TO THOSE INDIVIDUALS WHO PARTICIPATED IN
OUR BUILD A BOOK PROGRAM. THEY ARE:

Anonymous (14), Robert Abrams, Michael Ansara, Kathy Aponick,
Michael Anna de Armas, Jean Ball, Sally Ball, Clayre Benzadón,
Adrian Blevins, Laurel Blossom, Adam Bohannon, Betsy Bonner,
Patricia Bottomley, Lee Briccetti, Joel Brouwer, Susan Buttenwieser,
Anthony Cappo, Paul and Brandy Carlson, Dan Clarke, Mark Conway,
Elinor Cramer, Kwame Dawes, John Del Peschio,
Brian Komei Dempster, Patrick Donnelly, Lynn Emanuel,
Blas Falconer, Jennifer Franklin, John Gallaher, Reginald Gibbons,
Rebecca Kaiser Gibson, Dorothy Tapper Goldman, Julia Guez,
Naomi Guttman and Jonathan Mead, Forrest Hamer, Luke Hankins,
Yona Harvey, KT Herr, Karen Hildebrand, Carlie Hoffman,
Glenna Horton, Thomas and Autumn Howard, Catherine Hoyser,
Elizabeth Jackson, Linda Susan Jackson, Jessica Jacobs and Nickole
Brown, Lee Jenkins, Elizabeth Kanell, Nancy Kassell, Maeve Kinkead,
Victoria Korth, Brett Lauer and Gretchen Scott, Howard Levy,
Owen Lewis and Susan Ennis, Margaree Little, Sara London and
Dean Albarelli, Tariq Luthun, Myra Malkin, Louise Mathias,
Victoria McCoy, Lupe Mendez, Michael and Nancy Murphy,
Kimberly Nunes, Susan Okie and Walter Weiss, Cathy McArthur
Palermo, Veronica Patterson, Jill Pearlman, Marcia and
Chris Pelletiere, Sam Perkins, Susan Peters and Morgan Driscoll, Maya
Pindyck, Megan Pinto, Kevin Prufer, Martha Rhodes and Jean Brunel,
Paula Rhodes, Louise Riemer, Peter and Jill Schireson, Rob Schlegel,
Yoana Setzer, Soraya Shalforoosh, Mary Slechta, Diane Souvaine,
Barbara Spark, Catherine Stearns, Jacob Strautmann, Yerra Sugarman,
Arthur Sze and Carol Moldaw, Marjorie and Lew Tesser,
Dorothy Thomas, Rosalynde Vas Dias, Rushi Vyas, Martha Webster and
Robert Fuentes, Abby Wender and Rohan Weerasinghe,
Rachel Weintraub and Allston James, and Monica Youn.